BROTHERS
TO
ONE ANOTHER

BROTHERS
TO
ONE ANOTHER

The De La Salle Brothers
behind the Iron Curtain

ROMANIA
HUNGARY
CZECHOSLOVAKIA

GERARD RUMMERY FSC

LaSallian Education Services
Melbourne Australia

First published in 2011 by
LaSallian Education Services
1318 High St Malvern
Victoria 3144 Australia
tel +61 3 9824 8502
fax +61 3 9824 5229
www.lasallian.org.au

Cover image: Detail from the balustrade at the entrance of the Church of
St George the New, Bucharest
Design & production by David Lovell Publishing
Typeset in 11.5/17 Book Antiqua
Printed and bound in Australia by On-Demand Printing

National Library of Australia
Cataloguing-in-Publication card number
and ISBN: 978 0 9751148 5 8 (pbk.)

Contents

Foreword   vii

Preface   xi

1. My Background and Interest in This Work
   1969, 1986-1993   1

2. The Brothers in Romania after 1948   9

3. The Brothers in the Former Czechoslovakia
   after 1948   19

4. The Brothers in Hungary after 1948   29

5. The Heroic Struggle of the Romanian Brothers   35

6. In Romania: A Long Night that Lasted
   42 Years   55

7. Overview of the Czechoslovakia District   71

8. Some Remarkable Brothers   89

9. 'Being Brothers to One Another'   105

10. After 1990   119

Sources   128

Map showing Russia, the 'Iron Curtain', and the countries dealt with in this Memorandum.

Foreword

Between the end of the Second World War and 1990, the countries of Central and Eastern Europe were separated from Western Europe by what Winston Churchill referred to on 5 March 1946 as an 'iron curtain':

> From Stettin in the Baltic to Trieste in the Adriatic an iron curtain has descended over the Continent. Behind that line lie all the capitals of the ancient states of Central and Eastern Europe, Warsaw, Berlin, Prague, Vienna, Budapest, Belgrade, Bucharest and Sofia. All these famous cities and their populations around them lie in what I call the Soviet sphere, and all are subject in one way or another, not only to Soviet influence, but to a very high and in some cases increasing measure of control from Moscow.

In three of these countries, Romania, Czechoslovakia (since 1918 one country) and Hungary, the Brothers of the Christian Schools,[1] a lay teaching brotherhood of the Catholic Church, had long established schools and institutions that taught boys and young men. As Communist governments gradually took

---

[1] The Brothers of the Christian Schools – the De La Salle Brothers – were founded in France in 1680 as a lay religious congregation of the Catholic Church. Members who live in community under a nominated Director choose not to be ordained. Provinces in different parts of the world are the responsibility of an elected Provincial or Visitor.

over the control of each of these countries by 1948, the schools and institutions of the Brothers were taken over by the state, and the Brothers themselves had their schools closed and were usually forbidden to teach. In Czechoslovakia the Brothers, along with priests and dissidents, were put into concentration monasteries where they were required to carry out forced labour for many years. In Romania and Hungary, after the closure of their communities, the Brothers were required to find employment as best they could and to find a place to live. As their communities were now formally disbanded and any attempt to meet as formerly was punishable, each Brother had to decide whether or not he wished to continue to live as a member of the Brotherhood or whether he should seek formal dispensation from the vows he had taken and marry. In Romania, the continuing influence of individual Brothers with youth groups 1950-1958, eventually led the government to make an exhibition of four Brothers in a 'show trial' that condemned them to hard labour for 15 to 20 years along with other dissidents in the construction of a canal in the Danube Delta to improve river traffic with the Black Sea.

The history of each of these three countries shows that the initial success of the totalitarian governments was not lasting. In Hungary in October 1956 there was an almost spontaneous outburst of public anger against food shortages which led the prime minister to decide to leave the Warsaw Pact alliance to seek stronger contacts with the NATO and US alliance. On 4 November, however, this rebellion was brutally suppressed by Soviet soldiers and a minister favourable to Moscow was installed. In Prague in January 1968, the chief minister, Alexander Dubcek, brought down a series of reforms known as the 'Prague Spring', but this in turn was not lasting. By 1988, it was evident that reforms initiated by the 'Solidarity' movement in Poland were going to succeed, and in a series of upheavals across the 'Eastern Bloc', as it was called, the so-called 'Velvet Revolution' in Prague in November 1989 and civil unrest in East Germany saw the destruction of the Berlin Wall which from 1961 had divided East and West Germany. Events in Timisoara in western Romania in 1989 led to a popular uprising initiated from within the lower ranks of the Communist government that led to the capture and summary execution of the dictator Nicolae Ceaușescu and his wife on Christmas Day and the gradual establishment of a more humane government.

The narrative that follows chronicles the story of the Brothers in these three countries. It is based on original written accounts of what happened and on the efforts made by Brothers from outside these countries to support and encourage them.

Preface

'Being Brothers to One Another ...'

We have abundant documentation about many aspects of the lives and sufferings of the Brothers in Eastern Europe between 1948 and 1989. What is still lacking, however, is a general appreciation for the brotherly concern shown in so many practical ways by the Brothers themselves amid their own sufferings and the extraordinarily generous and sustained efforts made by successive Brothers Provincials of the Austrian District and by the General Council of the Institute during all these years.

My personal experiences in meeting Brothers in Hungary, Czech, Slovakia and Romania, usually in the company of a succession of Austrian Provincials, has often brought to my mind that special historical moment in the 1680s when the first disciples of Canon John Baptist de La Salle decided to call themselves 'Brothers', and defined their brotherhood as being 'Brothers to one another and older Brothers to the children' in their schools.

The first part of this anthropological cornerstone of the Brothers in the 1680s, 'being Brothers to one another', seems to me to be a perfect description and summary of what so many Brothers lived in Eastern Europe over more than fifty years. It is the significant title of the Memorandum that follows in these pages.

Why a Memorandum?

The original meaning of the word *memorandum* from Latin can range over 'something which (deserves to, should, must) be remembered'. It is worth remembering that the good men to be met with in the pages that follow, who were helping young people to be educated and to live Christian lives, were called 'criminals', 'bandits', 'robbers' and 'parasites' and treated as such; it is worth remembering that so many of these good men suffered cruelty, torture, forced labour and isolation for doing what they had unselfishly committed their lives to doing; it is worth remembering that in spite of all that was done to them, these good men still attempted to help others to live better lives; it is worth remembering that other men who called themselves 'Brothers' in solidarity with those who suffered deprivation of liberty and freedom of speech were prepared to risk their own security to do whatever could be done to alleviate their sufferings and to work towards the day when people enslaved under Communism would be free.

Brother Gerard Rummery
28 September 2010

NOTE

As Poland was originally part of the original Czechoslovakian District, the English Assistant Brother Richard McNamee made a number of visits after 1967. There were, however, practical difficulties in visiting by car, especially in obtaining transit visas to cross from Austria into Poland via Czech or Slovakia. It was eventually more practical to fly to Warsaw. After 1986, Brother Joseph Hendron, a member of the General Council, was responsible for liaison with Poland. The story of the Polish Brothers is not part of this document.

CHAPTER ONE

My Background and Interest in This Work 1969; 1986-1993

In July 1969 I was invited by Brother Charles Henry, Superior General, to accompany Brother Richard Allen McNamee to visit some of the Brothers in parts of Eastern Europe by car. The occasion for the visit at this time was that information had been received in Rome via a note from a former student of the Brothers, now a pilot with TAROM (Air Romania), that Brother Marcellin Joan Magui was now out of prison and staying at a certain address in Bucharest. It was important to make contact with him and if possible bring him some money as he would have no income.

I was due to begin post-graduate studies in England in September/October 1969, I was keen to see countries I had never seen, and I was the possessor of a new Australian passport with only one entry outside of Australia. What I did not know, but which became clear only some two to three kilometres from the border between Austria and Hungary, was that, as both the driver of the car, a young Austrian Brother, Walter Pingitzer and Brother Richard McNamee had had their luggage thoroughly searched in leaving Hungary in the previous October, I was to carry the money. Because of his duties in visiting English-speaking countries in Asia and Australia, Brother Richard's English passport was already almost half-filled with visas for many countries and therefore attracted close attention at the borders of countries behind the Iron Curtain. It fell to me, therefore, to carry a large sum of money in American dollars, while declaring only a much smaller amount. As a strategy this proved successful as my passport and declaration attracted little attention in crossing first into Hungary.

Hungary

In Hungary, we were able to visit the Auxiliary-Provincial, Brother Kolos Nagy, at Vesces, where he had lived with the parish priest for the past 18 years since the Brothers' schools had been closed by the Communist government. Brother Kolos, like many Hungarian Brothers I was later to meet, was a polyglot and spoke to us in excellent French. I was impressed by his deep faith and his gratitude for the visit and for the money we were able to leave with him.

Our next visit with Brother Kolos was in Budapest itself, not far from where the Brothers had conducted an important primary and secondary school where everything was taught in Hungarian and German. Our visit was to a family whose sons had been pupils in the school and which had given lodging to two older Brothers, a Brother Miklos and another whose name I have forgotten, who were unable to escape from Hungary with younger Brothers during the 1956 revolution. I can recall Brother Miklos asking me if I had seen the Soviet 'fish'. As I looked puzzled, he pointed to the monument the Soviets had set up on the hill facing us which showed a soldier with both arms extended holding a banner. 'You see', said Brother Miklos, 'he's been fishing and caught a big fish!' I remember thinking just how resilient these Brothers are.

It was with this family that Brother Kolos usually met with the other Brothers on Sundays. The family name was Simon, and the father, champion motor driver in Hungary for seven successive years, had never been allowed to compete abroad as the family was Jewish, the surviving members of a Jewish family most of whom had been victims of the Holocaust. The two Brothers found some form of employment as unskilled labourers: it was the practice in all Communist countries to forbid the Brothers to live in community and to teach. These two Brothers were to live with the Simon family and to die there after 1972. This family was subsequently affiliated to the Institute.[2] Years later, when I saw the film *Sunshine* (1999), the story of the Sonnenschein family, I realised how closely it parallelled the story of the Simon family.

Czechoslovakia

We crossed into what was then Czechoskovkia via the border close to Bratislava. Here we were to make contact if possible with the acting Provincial, Ján Rybanski, who had trained in French in Lembecq-les-Halles in Belgium, and afterwards in English at Dover and had, like a number of his fellow-countrymen, become a missionary and taught in English in Sri Lanka for over 20 years. Returning to his native Slovakia after the war, he suffered the same fate as all the Brothers when the schools were closed, the communities dissolved and many Brothers were consigned to work camps. He was fortunate that the Communists, wishing to profit by his language skills, employed him

---

[2] Officially regarded as honorary members of the Brotherhood.

as an interpreter and translator in a chemical factory that sold products into the West. Because of this he was given an apartment of which we had the address, but previous experience had shown that his mail and phone were supervised by the authorities so that it was not possible to let him know we were coming. We decided to visit his apartment on the chance that he might be there, and, if not, to leave a note saying simply where we could be contacted.

Even after more than 40 years, I still have a vivid memory of taking the lift to the fifth floor of the apartment block where Brother Ján lived. In coming out of the lift, there were four apartments, three with lights under the door and sounds of people inside, but Brother Ján's apartment showed no light. When we knocked on the door, the lights of the other three apartments were immediately extinguished and suddenly there was no more sound. We left a note under the door indicating the phone number of the hotel where we were staying, signed as SJB, which he would recognise through previous experience as a form of contact from outside the country. The following day we were able to meet with him for a short time at dinner in the hotel and give him money for the isolated Brothers who had no regular work or who were living with their families.

Romania

The following day we entered Romania from the north. I had easily obtained a visa in London to travel to the Black Sea to holiday there for a few days, passing via Brazov in the Carpathians and then on to Bucharest. On the morning after our arrival in Bucharest we found the address for Brother Marcellin and I was sent in to ask for him. The surly doorkeeper, after I had given his family name, pointed as I thought up the stairs but as I was going to ascend, he pointed to the angle made by the staircase with the floor – the broom cupboard! After I knocked, out came a smiling little man who immediately greeted me in French telling me to say nothing more. Once outside he greeted my travelling companions quickly and then asked us to meet him in ten minutes time, sitting in the back seat in the nearby Latin-rite church in Belu next to the Catholic cemetery. True to his word, he knelt behind us and a short conversation in French was conducted without our turning round to face him. He assumed or knew that the church was bugged. He quickly made arrangements for us to meet with him later that day while he arranged places for short meetings on the following day with three other Brothers who were in Bucharest.

We were able to arrange for Brother Augustin, who lived in the bishop's house, to act as custodian for most of the money we had brought. But we also asked each Brother if he could make use of US dollars without compromising his safety. This was one of the most memorable moments of the whole trip for me. Brother Marcellin, consigned to forced labour on the notorious Danube canal for some years, imprisoned subsequently on three separate occasions for teaching religion in families, was at first hesitant to take any dollars because, as he said, 'They're dangerous and can be traced.' Finally, however, he asked if we could give him 18 single dollars. When it was suggested that he could have much more, he insisted on $18. When asked why, he replied simply that with this sum he thought he would be able to buy a bicycle and this would enable him to teach in two families each night.

This matter-of-fact statement still remains one of those moments when I felt an overwhelming surge of emotion for the courage and faith of this man who believed so strongly in his vocation as Brother that, barely out of prison, he was still prepared to risk his freedom again because of what he saw as his ministry.

After these two days we decided not to continue to the Black Sea but return via Hungary to avoid having to exit by the border where we had declared our intention to go to the Black Sea. On leaving Bucharest, however, our car had to stop at a railway crossing where a long line of oil trains cross over the road. We were the first car and had no idea just how long the crossing would take, so we left our motor running until someone in a following car came and spoke to us in French explaining that the delay would be about 20 minutes. As it was very hot weather, I got out of the car and sat down on the side of a nearby stream where the man who had spoken with us came and sat down beside me. After initial questions about where I was from, he explained that he was an engineer travelling to an international conference in Paris. He explained, however, that he was not allowed to take his wife and children with him, because, as he said, 'I have to leave hostages.' Then, more cautiously, he told me that he could not say anything critical about the government even to his wife, because, and these words are etched in my memory, 'In this country it is not good to know anything about anyone else.'

It was no surprise when we came to the border with Hungary that we were asked why we had not gone to the Black Sea, a clear indication of just how closely we had been monitored. Mindful of the difficulties encountered by Brothers Richard and Walter in the previous year at the Hungarian/Austrian border, we returned via Slovakia and crossed at Bratislava into Austria. Even here there was some question as to whether my transit visa was still valid and we were detained for some hours. When it seemed that paying a few more dollars would solve the problem, we were cleared to re-enter Austria, aided by the gesture of the handsome Brother Walter presenting a bouquet of flowers we had been given to the young woman lieutenant who was in charge of our detention.

This was a most memorable and life-changing trip for me. I was as yet unaware that after 1986, as an elected member of the General Council of the Brothers and the only one with some limited competence in German because of my doctoral studies, I would be asked to be the liaison between the Council and the Brothers of Eastern Europe for the next seven years. From 1986, I was able through frequent visits with Austrian Brothers, especially Brother Bruno Schmid, to renew my acquaintance with Brothers I had met some 17 years previously and would live with them the joy of the lifting of the Iron Curtain at the end of 1989. I was privileged to listen to many personal accounts, especially after 1990, during an assembly of the survivors in Vienna. It is because of these unexpected and life-changing events in my life that this Memorandum is written. It is a duty that I feel I owe to my Brothers who remained faithful to their calling in spite of all the unexpected turnings that they encountered in their lives.

CHAPTER TWO

The Brothers in Romania after 1948

T he Brothers came to Romania first from Vienna in 1861 at the request of the Latin-rite archbishop and opened a school in Bucharest. After 1921, when a substantial section of eastern Hungary became part of Romania, Hungarian Brothers continued to maintain their schools and became part of the Romanian province. In 1948 there were some 20 Brothers serving in the three schools in Bucharest, with eight Hungarian Brothers in Satu Mare.

The overall chronicle of the Brothers in Romania after 1948, and the particular stories of those who were formally condemned by military tribunals of the Inland Security (*Securitate*) in 1958, can be followed in chapters 5 and 6 from the detailed accounts written some years later by Brothers Dominic Bernhard and Brother Tiberiù Ratu who survived prison terms and forced labour with other Brothers in the Danube Delta. Before following their individual stories, however, here is the general chronology of events between 1948 and the collapse of the Ceauşescu regime in December 1989.

On 2 August 1948, the 20 Brothers were concluding their annual retreat in Bucharest when the Directors of the three schools were summoned by the government authorities to be told that all schools were to be nationalised. The directive stated that the keys of the schools were to be handed over immediately and the communities vacated. The Brothers were given an hour to collect their personal effects only, as everything else was to be left in the schools. As they gathered in the street with their belongings, the Brothers were told they were henceforth to occupy the second storey of the Latin-rite bishop's residence, where older seminarians had previously lived. They were told that they could seek employment as teachers if anyone wanted them, or else they would have to seek some kind of employment as best they could, by qualifying as workmen. While they lived in the same building, they were not to wear their religious habits nor were they to form a community.

The Jesuits and Franciscans were allowed to continue to work in parishes but as individuals and all forms of religious dress were henceforth forbidden. Similar regulations were applied at the same time to religious congregations of women. The so-called 'English Sisters'[3] had to give up their school in the city but were allowed to go as a group to occupy their vacation house on the outskirts of the city.

Three Brothers were employed in the Nunciature as secretaries, translators and producers of materials for church ceremonies and liturgies. Theoretically, at least, this office had diplomatic immunity and remained open for the next two years under the leadership of Archbishop Patrick O'Hara, a US citizen. Some Brothers living in the major seminary took the opportunity to improve their professional qualifications as teachers. Other Brothers found employment as best they could, some by seeking qualifications as workers in various traditional occupations. This was not so easy. Anyone seeking to become qualified had to become a member of a union, to attend meet-

---

[3] A congregation founded by Mary Ward for educating girls.

ings which included Communist propaganda, and to submit to direction which often had nothing to do with the skills needed. In practice, therefore, most Brothers, at the request of parents of their former pupils, began teaching in families. This teaching, again usually at the request of the parents, gradually included also religious instruction. The fact that a large number of the Brothers under the leadership of Brother Bonifazius, an Austrian and Auxiliary-Provincial, were living in the same building, seeing one another at various times of the day, exchanging news at meal times, meant that many of the traditional community structures were in fact maintained. The catechetical work was extended to parishes and gradually some very strong youth groups of young men and women were set up. Brother Tiberiù's account describes this steady growth and its consequences:

> After the Helsinki Conference,[4] it looked as if the clouds would clear up. The Brothers returned to their residence in the former major seminary and restarted their catechism classes in five parishes where every Sunday some 300 Catholics would gather. This was not to the liking of the Communist authorities. They would say to their colleagues: 'You can't even manage to organise Communist youth meetings, and yet this handful of religious teachers fills its halls every Sunday.' Former students and friends warned the Brothers that trouble was brewing. Brother Bonifazius remained calm and continued to inspire his Brothers to be faithful and trust in God.[5]

In October 1948, the very year in which it celebrated the 250th year of its declaration of unity with the Vatican, the Greek-Catholic Church had been forcibly integrated with the

---

[4] It was thought that this conference would bring a measure of religious freedom.

[5] See chapter 5.

Orthodox Church. All of its bishops and any priests who in any way attempted to resist were imprisoned. The Communist Party Secretary, Gheorghiu-Dej, had already further indicated in 1948 that the obstacle to 'true democracy' in Romania was the Latin-rite Catholic Church because 'the new constitution will not allow Catholic citizens to be submissive to the directives of a foreign ruler; it will not allow Romanians to be tempted by the American "golden calf", at whose feet the Vatican wants to bring its faithful.'[6]

While the Nunciature remained open, news of the arrests and suspicious deaths of some of the Greek-Catholic bishops in prison and the mysterious disappearance of some priests had been sent to Rome. The fact that Vatican Radio had broadcast this information had so angered the Communist authorities that they ignored the diplomatic immunity of the Nunciature and broke into it. On 19 July 1950, following the escape of the Nuncio, a US citizen, through the advice and the help of the CIA prior to his formal expulsion, the three Brothers who worked in the Nunciature, Julius, Tarcisiu and Justin, and a Sister, were arrested. In an attempt to break the very efficient network of the Nunciature, all those arrested were tortured and eventually condemned to varying sentences from 14 to 20 years of imprisonment and hard labour.

Four More Brothers Arrested

Eight years after the arrests of the staff of the Nunciature, some Brothers were now living in families and with former students, keeping contact with one another as best they could, but more and more conscious that there were spies being introduced

---

[6] *The Calvary of Romania* by Robert Royal, Catholic World Report, March 2000, p. 3.

among their pupils. Things came to a head on 17 August 1958, when Brothers Dominic, Tiberiù, Florentin and Valeriù had gone from Bucharest with some 20 students to a holiday house in Sinaia in the Carpathian mountains. Brothers Dominic and Tiberiù were arrested by the *Securitate*, and taken first to Brazov where they were handcuffed overnight and interrogated the next day. They were first accused of being Jesuits but this was obviously meant to be a distraction because the subsequent interrogation showed that they had indeed been spied upon and their words reported. They were then driven to Bucharest and imprisoned along with Brothers Augustin and Florentin, arrested in Bucharest. In December 1958 they were made the object of show trials and condemned. Brothers Dominic and Tiberiù received sentences of 20 years with loss of citizenship for ten years, the two other Brothers 15 years, and the two former students, ten years.

Brother Tiberiù's account of the conditions in prison awaiting trial is graphic in its detail:

> There were 110 of us in a room measuring 11 metres by 10. There was one window boarded up with planks, nailed down on the outside to prevent the prisoners from looking out. In one corner, to attract the rats, there were four buckets (there was no lavatory). The buckets were free once or twice a day. No one could stay close to the window. It was absolutely forbidden. We had to lie on our sides, pressed together like sardines. Often and most of the time, the most recent arrivals would have to sleep sitting on the buckets that served as lavatories.[7]

Following their condemnation and loss of citizenship, the Brothers were subjected to forced labour in the Danube Delta

---

[7] Institute *Bulletin*, No. 235, September 1991. See chapter 6.

where a huge earth dam and canal to the Black Sea, 17 metres high and 25 kilometres in length, was being built over many years by perhaps as many as 80,000 prisoners.

Brother Dominic gives a vivid description of 50 men being transported for three and a half days and nights in a cattle wagon, all sources of light covered up, no knowledge of where they were being taken, a water bucket and a toilet bucket in the corner, before being taken by boat to an island in the Danube where a portly officer stood on a table and gave the following instructions:

> Here you must work … This is the way to freedom. There is no compassion on this island. Don't even think of escaping for that is certain death. For every ten men there is one soldier with a rifle and a ferocious dog. Your work is this dam. Every day three cubic metres of earth are to be dug up and taken to the dam. If you don't do this, you will get the *bastinado* or you'll be put in the hunger bunker. And think of my final words: *work* and *discipline!*[8]

Brother Dominic describes the living conditions as follows:

> Our sleeping room? A brushwood sheepfold. 250 rusty iron beds, three storeys high; palliasses, straw pillows, old, shreds of cloth; two per bed, or sometimes five for two beds; the stable was so airy that sparrows flew through the roof; mice swarmed in our pockets and shoes. Such was our home for a year. Woe betide us when the winter surprised us.
>
> As brigades we were awoken at 6.00 am, given about 400 grams of maize bread, our ration for the day. This thing had the shape and form of burnt tile, and from then on this 'Kirpik' was referred to as Turkish brick. Each man had also his 'Sarsana', the Turkish name for a bread sack. Everything

---

[8] See chapter 5 and *Krähen und Pelikane*, p. 9.

was wrapped up in an old shirt; in it we also carried our metal plate and our spoon. For washing we were rationed to a half litre of water from the Danube, which stood in containers in front of our stable.

We were ready to go. With us there were armed soldiers and wolfhounds. A sergeant loudly proclaimed like a prayer the same message every morning for the whole year, before the march began: 'During the march keep your head down, look at the ground in front of you and don't look up. Anyone who steps out of line will be shot without being challenged.'[9]

One of the ironies of the success of this extraordinary project, as Brother Dominic's memoir *Krähen und Pelikane* records, was that it was regularly reported in the world press as the work of 'volunteers'.[10]

In April 1959, the remaining nine 'free' Brothers in Bucharest were brought together in the Military Prefecture in Bucharest and were divided into three separate groups of three. They were assigned three different locations, each a long distance from the capital, under what was called 'obligatory residence', with the right to move only within a three kilometre radius of where they were confined. In fact, this helped them maintain some form of community life but obliged them to find work to support themselves. This was, until 1964 at least, the 'official' end of many of the pastoral activities of the Brothers since 1948.

Brother Dominic survived the forced labour on the dam because of a political change. In 1964, after Nicolae Ceauşescu's access to power, there was international pressure for him to offer an amnesty which allowed Brother Dominic's sisters in Germany and the United States to apply through the Red Cross for

---

[9] *Krähen und Pelikane*, p. 11.
[10] ibid, p. 13.

his release. When this had been granted, he was able to travel to Vienna and, along with the repatriated Austrian Brothers Bonifazius and Sylvester, bring at first-hand the certain news about what had happened to the Brothers, those who had died and where the survivors now were.

Brother Tiberiù lasted only two years at the Danube work, came close to dying several times in hospital in Constantia, and was eventually returned to the infamous prison of Gherla where he was occupied in making tables. It was only in August 1964 that, under the amnesty, he was finally released from prison – but not from supervision – and eventually made his way to his home. He writes of this meeting with his mother:

> For a long time I had thought she was dead. I was very attached to my mother as she had been largely responsible for my vocation to the Brothers. My meeting with her was very moving both for her and for me ... For a long time she wept in my arms, repeating over and over again, 'My dear child, my dear child.' And I wept with her. Everyone in the house did, we all wept for joy![11]

He was not, however, free to leave and do whatever he wished. He was still under the control of the *Securitate*. He therefore sought out the Brothers in Bucharest, but after a short meeting only three who had relatives in and around Bucharest could stay there, without being able to form a community. Because he was still known and registered as a Brother, he was obliged to find work but the only work offered him at first was in the mines. He began this work, but his friends and former pupils found him a position as a librarian, Some of his family lived locally and he was able to live with them, first for

---

[11] See chapter 6

three months in a room with four young children and then for the next three and a half years before he eventually found a single room to stay in. During all this time, he received help from some of the Hungarian Brothers[12] some 700 kilometres away to the west near the Hungarian border, who paid his fare to come and stay with them for a short time every two months.

The freeing of Brother Dominic and the return to Vienna of two Austrian Brothers, Brothers Bonifazius and Sylvester, who had been living since April 1959 in compulsory detention with a Franciscan community at Estelnic, prompted the activity of the Austrian Brothers to visit and bring help in many different ways from 1965 to 1989. Meanwhile, Brother Liebhard as Provincial had already made his first visit to Estelnic before the Brothers were allowed to return to Austria. This topic is treated in a later chapter.

The translations of Brother Tiberiù's condemnation and the complete text of his written account are given in chapter 6 and referred to in the Sources (see p. 128). There is a complete translation of Brother Dominic's formal account, written in Vienna 1966. Excerpts from two other of his documents are acknowledged within the text.

Brother Dominic's writings put us in touch with a natural poet. In the midst of the cruel work in the Danube Delta, he still marvels at the birds and the importance of 'Mother Danube' giving life to her children. Having just heard his condemnation to 20 years forced labour, he is vividly conscious of the children outside playing and of the birds singing.

---

[12] By a stroke of the pen in 1921, as a part of the Versailles agreement, some 3,000,000 Hungarians became Romanians in western Romania.

Prison Terms Served by Romanian Brothers

Imprisonment

Brother Tarcisiù and Brother Justin: 15 years
Brothers Dominic, Tiberiù, Augustin, Florentin: 6 years

House Arrest

Brothers Engelhard and Marcellin: 7 years
Brother Valentin: 5 years

Forced Labour/House Arrest

Brothers Damian, Atanasiu and Christian: 5 years

Forced Labour

Brother Valeriù: 2 years

CHAPTER THREE

The Brothers in the Former Czechoslovakia after 1948

The union of Czechoslovakia was part of the Versailles settlement of 1918, and the subsequent separation of Czech and Slovakia is once again a reality. The account that follows will treat the events that led to the Brothers losing all their institutions in both countries, to the closure of communities and the confinement of many in forced labour camps, especially in the construction of the Klicava Dam to the west of Prague. We are fortunate in having two different account, the first written at my request by the then 'unofficial' Visitor, Brother Ján Rybansky, around 1988, and a second longer account in French entitled *Historical Essay on the Suppression and Reconstruction of the District of Czechoslovakia*, written around 1993 by the then Delegate to the newly-created Delegation, Brother Vincent Gottwald. Citations in the present text are based on the complete account found in chapter 7.

The Night of 4 May 1950

As the District of Czechoslovakia in 1950 included Poland, there were 16 communities, 12 schools, three teachers' colleges, a novitiate and a scholasticate, with a total of 121 Brothers. All of this, however, was suppressed, along with all other religious communities, during the night of 4 May 1950. The Communist military and police invaded all the religious communities, giving the religious time to take only their personal effects before being taken to concentration camps which had been prepared beforehand. Members of the same community were often deliberately taken to different places, with Czechs frequently being imprisoned in monasteries and convents in Slovakia and Slovakians in monasteries and convents in Czech. Our Brothers were imprisoned in five places in Slovakia and in four places in the Czech provinces of Moravia and Bohemia.

The Brothers, along with brothers and priests from other congregations, were forbidden to wear their religious habits and were given working clothes. Sometimes they were confined for a short time where they were captured, but before long they were taken to designated camps and put to heavy manual work such as building and repairing roads. A large number of Brothers were sent to construct a massive earth dam at Klicava to serve the city of Prague. People sent to build this dam were told in typical Communist propaganda, 'You priests and religious have been parasites in our society: now we will show you how to work!' President Zapotocky had the good grace years later in opening the dam some years earlier than had been expected, to say: 'We thought of teaching you how to work, but you have taught us.' This dam popularly known as the 'Dam of the Religious', was later called the 'Model Dam'. One of the Brothers, Oldrich Elías, became a foreman at this construction site, but when he refused to become a taskmaster to force the other workers to reach their quota, he was warned and threatened and finally sent to the Zeliva monastery, renowned for its harshness. Here, in attempting to send a note to his parents by passing it though the fence to a passer-by, he was detected and imprisoned for two weeks in a dark and wet cellar, living only on bread and water. When Brother Oldrich contracted pneumonia, the camp doctor declared that the prisoner was likely to die, but the commandant insisted that he must serve his full sentence. He did, but was weakened and eventually died in the Klastor-pod-Znievom camp in the presence of other Brothers.

Certain Brothers received heavy prison sentences because of information preciously collected about their activities. Brother Arnold Bis, the then Provincial, was given an eight-year sentence because he was accused of calling an 'illegal assembly' in April, when he had called the Brothers together to decide what to do if the communities were threatened with closure. We know also of Brother Filip Paluch's seven-year sentence, Brother Rudolf Pasko's four years, and that of Brother Augustin Rybansky, brother of Ján and also a former missionary in Sri Lanka, sentenced for three years.

Malicious Propaganda

Because the Brothers' schools and establishments were highly appreciated by the parents and friends of their pupils, there was an attempt made after the removal of the Brothers from their residences on 5 May 1950 to invite local people to visit the residences where particularly explicit pornography had been placed. Brother Ján's account says simply,

> Strange activities in the Brothers' rooms roused the curiosity of the Bojná people, and when they ceased, the Brothers in Mocenok [i.e. already imprisoned] had to line up day after day and 'confess' that they had pornography in their rooms. But the lining up ceased all of a sudden. 'What has happened?' asked the annoyed Brothers of one another. The

answer came from Bojná. Obscene paintings had been hung in their rooms in Bojná and then tentatively shown to people who indignantly told the evil-doers what they thought of them, for they had seen the Brothers' rooms many times.

The invasion of the main training house at Mocenok on the night of 4 May had already been prepared to discredit the morals of the Brothers. Brother Ján's account is again quite revealing.

> There was much talk about arrests during the evening recreation, but 'no danger for the Brothers for the time being' was the general opinion. Then like lightning, an absolute certainty struck a responsible Brother: 'They will come tonight.' After night prayers he hurried to Brother Visitor. Result: novices, scholastics, and Brothers with annual vows were told to pack and be off by 10 pm at the latest.
>
> In the dead of night, secret police, militiamen, protected by police and the military, broke into the Brothers' rooms, roused the quietly sleeping Brothers, gathered them against a wall in absolute silence while they ransacked the house. They were furious to find that the young were gone and wanted them back, but no addresses were given them.
>
> The young Brothers were spared the brutal arrest of the professed Brothers, and later, the seductions organised for seminarians and young religious through pretty but shameless girls.

There was one clear aim in the minds of the authorities. If the Catholic schools were closed and if the members of the religious communities were dispersed, mixed up with other religious or with ordinary people, and forbidden to assemble together in the future, they would have a free rein in developing an education system based on Marxist-Leninist principles. If, in addition, these religious, women or men, were kept locked away in the various monasteries and convents of concentration, a whole generation would grow up without their influence.

1950-1968

The dissolution of the communities, the separation of many Brothers from one another in different concentration camps and in different forms of forced labour, effectively destroyed the cohesion of the District. When Brothers who had not received prison sentences were freed from the work camps, each had to find a place to work and to live. Some returned to their families or older ones to their relatives. Brother Provincial Arnost, still under supervision, was moved from one place to another and eventually was cared for along with another elderly Brother, Vavrinec Jurak, by women religious. Two Slovak Brothers, Josef Dlouhy and Frantisek Demeter, were sent to run the farm at the famous Cistercian monastery of Osek in Bohemia, where religious women from 51 different congregations were confined, as the intention of the authorities was to make it as difficult as possible for these women to find support for one another from members of the same congregation.[13]

Communication was difficult, with the result that very few Brothers knew where their former community members now were. The supervision and control by the secret police and local authority – for example, obtaining a ticket to travel usually required seeking permission – was so efficient that most Brothers found themselves living alone and earning their own living as best they could. Without any regular form of communication, the sense of being part of a community gradually died out until the famous Prague Spring of 1968.

---

[13] See the DVD *Interrupted Lives*, a study of Catholic Sisters under European Communism through interviews with survivors.

A number of professed Brothers during this time, finding themselves completely isolated from any form of contact with the Institute, took advice about dispensation from their vows from bishops or priests whom they trusted, and decided to marry. Younger members, whose periods of temporary profession were now ended, were of course free to decide their own future.

After 1968

Seizing the temporary opportunity offered by the Prague Spring of 1968, Brother Vincent Gottwald, a native of Moravia, former missionary in Sri Lanka and at the time working as archivist at the University of Bethlehem, made a visit to his homeland. He was able to move freely, aided by the fact (as he discovered to his amusement and advantage) that his family name in his passport was the same as that of the former Communist leader and President, Clement Gottwald. In July, Brother Vincent was able to bring together some 18 Brothers for a meeting at his family home in Tupecy in Moravia. This became, in fact, a kind of 'chapter' at which Brother Vincent was able to share news of the important General Chapter of the Brothers in Rome in 1966-1967, and, in return, the Brothers were able to share news of other Brothers of whom they had heard news, and to share addresses.

As the former Brother Visitor had died, the 18 Brothers decided unanimously to elect as Provincial Brother Ján Rybansky, who because of his language skills in French and English, had employment as a translator in a chemical firm. This position guaranteed him an apartment and a good salary. He was able to continue to act as Provincial from 1968 to 1990. It was most significant that one of the important decisions of the group was that of creating a common fund where the Brothers who had employment and some financial security tried to help support the older Brothers who relied on a state pension or those who for various reasons did not qualify for a state pension. Brothers were encouraged to open savings accounts in banks so that money could readily be available to meet the unexpected needs of others, such as sickness, medicines and funeral expenses for those who had no pension. This measure alone renewed bonds of brotherhood among men who were not able to meet. Brother Ján undertook to keep in touch with Brothers as discreetly as possible, especially after the savage Russian suppression of the Dubcek Spring.

I recall still my first visit with Brothers Bruno and Ján to Bojná in 1988 where the classic statue of John Baptist de La Salle, standing at one end of the property, had become isolated because a turning circle for a bus bay had been built that separated the statue from the property. Over the years the appearance of the statue had gradually deteriorated. Some of the enterprising former students who lived nearby brought a motion to the local council pointing out that the statue of a man 'who had first taught the children of the proletariat' needed to be upgraded. Such a demand in the right words had the desired effect so when I stated how impressed I was to see the statuary in such good condition, there were smiles all around.

Brother Ján kept in touch by making use of public transport for short weekend visits, and by a longer four-week journey to keep in touch with about 30 Brothers during the summer vacation. It was in the summer visits that he shared whatever money he had been sent with families who were looking after an aged Brother. After his compulsory retirement in 1975, he was able to move more freely, even to being able to obtain permission to visit Rome where he attended three weeks of the Institute's 1976

General Chapter. But he was always conscious that his mail, telephone and visits were being monitored and, for that reason, preferred to have few visitors from outside of the country. As proof that this concern was not imaginary, he smiles as he recalls that, after the collapse of Communism by late 1989, he was spoken to one day by a stranger in the street, who admitted to having followed him frequently, and then asked him if it was true that he was really 'a secret Jesuit'.

After the Velvet Revolution of November 1989

Following the restoration of religious freedom in November 1989, the General Council of the Brothers in Rome decided to re-establish the Institute as a 'Delegation', that is a structure where a president appointed by the Superior General was responsible for the overall organisation of a new sector. Brother Vincent Gottwald was appointed as Delegate at the end of January 1990 and immediately took up residence at his family home in Tupecy in Moravia. Brother Vincent, working closely with Brother Ján Rybanski, worked tirelessly for the next three years in establishing new communities, opened negotiations about the possible return of properties formerly owned by the Brothers and to which they had title, and eventually established an administrative centre and a Delegation Council.

'A Brother Helped by a Brother'

Perhaps the most striking aspect of the 1968 meeting of the 18 Brothers at Tupecy was their decision to try to help those other Brothers who were less fortunately placed as regards a regular salary or a pension. This was a clear recognition of their shared brotherhood. Their unanimous decision to share what little they had with their Brothers with whom they had been out of contact for the past 18 years was proof that they were indeed prepared to be 'Brothers to one another', even if they could not meet to share other community bonds.[14]

---

[14] In 1988, for example, I was able to spend the night in the apartment of Brother Hanuska, a train driver in the Prague Metro, who regularly contributed part of his salary to this common fund.

CHAPTER FOUR

The Brothers in Hungary after 1948

The story of the Brothers in Hungary since the first foundations from Vienna in 1894 when the Austro-Hungarian empire existed has been told in a series of detailed articles written and published by Brother Severin Hegedüs in various numbers of the Austrian District's *Rundbrief* between 1989 and 1991. This account is based on these articles. There were over 30 Brothers working in Hungary in 1946.

During the siege of Budapest in the Second World War, around Christmas 1944, the Brothers' school, St Josef's Educational Institution in Budapest XII, played an important role not only in sheltering the community members but also in providing a refuge for up to 60 members of Jewish families who were in danger of being deported. Brother Severin's first-hand account in *Rundbrief* (1990, No. 1, pp. 11-16) of the way in which the Brothers sheltered these families and managed to find food for them is its own tribute to the Brothers themselves, for all these families survived. The account also mentions how the Brothers accepted into their community a German officer, a Brother whose family name was Aigulf, clad him in the Brothers' traditional habit and at an appropriate moment, gave him Brother

Severin's own teaching certificate as an identity card, and thus enabled him to escape to Germany.

The school on the Buda hillside facing towards the Danube suffered extensive damage during the siege of Budapest by the Russians. Brother Severin, who was there in the community, states that it received between 200-250 hits from artillery and had 190 windows broken. The school was gradually re-opened in April 1945 with four classrooms and after 1946 different sections were repaired and the school expanded, largely with the help of local families and friends. This rebuilding was done also with the financial help of various international institutions from Sweden and the United Nations, with family help coming from the Brothers in Belgium (also repairing war-damaged buildings) and from the District of San Francisco. Steady progress was made, so that in April 1948 Cardinal József Mindszenty was able to visit the completed repair work and address the students.

On 17 June, however, following the end of the school year in June, a decree of the Hungarian government nationalised all Catholic schools. In the last week of June, members of a government commissioned arrived to make an inventory of everything in the school. Three Brothers had to accompany the members of this commission to all the different parts of the school, the boarding section and the 13 rooms of the Brothers' community. It seemed that the Brothers were to be allowed to remain in their residence but everything associated with the school was to be taken over by others. A lay director already teaching in the school was at first installed but quickly replaced after a month by another former teacher, who in turn was also replaced by someone named from outside the school. A separate director of the hostel and boarding section was named.

As the Brothers were at first to remain in their residence,

a separate wall was to be built that separated them from the school but gave students access to the Brothers' chapel. The authorities, however, countermanded this adaptation. Similar restrictions were placed over the Brothers' school and hostel at Homok. As Cardinal Mindszenty had forbidden religious to take positions in state institutions, the Brothers had to find various positions in offices and churches to gain their livelihood. The Brothers, isolated in their community in Budapest, were supported in various ways by families such as the Simon family, already referred to in the opening chapter, who had had their children in the school.

Eventually, in June 1950, the Brothers were directed to vacate their Budapest community and hand the keys over to the school director. This presented serious challenges. Some of the older members had no family to go to, the Cardinal's prohibition against the Brothers taking employment in state schools still stood, and there were various sacred objects, relics and statues to be placed in safe keeping. As indicated in the opening chapter, two Brothers were invited to live with the Simon family and did so until their deaths. Overall, the Brothers became dispersed as individuals until two of the younger members profited by the popular uprising in Budapest in 1956 to escape to Austria.

15 August 1949

Meanwhile, four Brothers and two scholastics[15] in the scholasticate community at Szeged, after celebrating the feast of the Assumption in the cathedral, returned to their residence to find government officials awaiting them. They were told that they were to leave the residence at once, taking their posses-

---

[15] Scholastics were student Brothers completing university studies after having been accepted into the Brotherhood.

sions with them to a large Franciscan cloister where the Father Guardian had been told to prepare rooms for them. They were able to obtain transport for everything they could carry, including an extensive library, and were given generous space in the Franciscan cloister. The books were eventually stored in the cathedral tower and the Brothers adjusted themselves to living in the cloister and taking their midday meal with the Franciscans in a nearby Caritas Centre. Brother Severin contacted the local bishop to register an official protest at the way in which their house had been taken over.

This state of affairs was suddenly interrupted at midnight on 10 June 1950. State police and officials forced the gatekeeper to open the house and all the occupants were given ten minutes to pack a small bag and be ready to leave. Although Brother Severinus attempted to take important Institute ownership documents with him, he was ordered to leave them behind. By three o'clock, all the occupants of the cloister were told to leave their possessions in a police wagon and they were packed into another, accompanied by four guards, two policemen and two members of the State police. They were forbidden to speak to one another. They were uncertain where they were being taken but realised they were travelling in the direction of Debrezin, and wondered whether they were being taken to Russia. They were given one stop to relieve themselves but otherwise travelled almost 12 hours before they found themselves, along with other men from religious congregations, in the garden of a Franciscan cloister in Debrezin. For the next 50 days or so, they were left to themselves, but forbidden to wear any religious habits or to hold any kind of meetings. There was a general feeling that they would all eventually be transported into Russia.

Brother Severin tells of being called to the office where he was interrogated for a long time by two women Communist officers about his understanding of Communism. He emphasised that his understanding was that it had something to do with helping the poor, and so was told he would be freed if he had relatives living in the country. Having given the address of his sister in Budapest, he was freed and eventually found a room to live in in the XII district of Budapest, with which of course he was familiar. Here he found employment as a book-keeper with a small salary, made acquaintance with some of the Catholic families he already knew in the area and gradually took the evening meal with various families who wished him to instruct their children in religion. During the national uprising of 1956 he was able to visit the Auxiliary-Provincial Brother Kolos in Vecses where he lived with the parish priest. While some of the younger Brothers were able to escape to Austria before the popular uprising was brutally repressed by the Russians, Brother Severin had to wait until 3 October 1959 when, with the help of another sister living in West Germany, he was allowed to go to Austria where he joined the community at Strebersdorf in Vienna.

Although some forms of contact with the Brothers remaining in Hungary were maintained and occasional visits were made, the young Brothers could not renew their vows, the older Brothers gradually died and everything came to a standstill until after the collapse of Communism in 1989. The re-launching of the school in Budapest XII after 1990 is dealt with in chapter 10.

(Material for this chapter has been taken mainly from *Rundbrief*, 1990. No. 1, pp.11-16 and *Rundbrief*, 1991, No. 1, pp. 17-21.)

CHAPTER FIVE

The Heroic Struggle of the Romanian Brothers

*B*rother Dominic Bernhard, born in 1913 on the shores of the Black Sea in what was then Romania, was a pupil of the Brothers from 1921-1932 in Bucharest. After university studies and military service he joined the Brothers in 1936 and made his novitiate in Austria. Gifted in languages, he taught German, French and English at the school St Josef in Bucharest where he had been a pupil. He has left us three important texts about his arrest, imprisonment, condemnation and forced labour in the Danube Delta. His first text, written in Vienna at Christmas 1965, just some months after he was freed, is an episodic, almost impressionistic and at times a highly poetic piece of writing about the forced labour on the Danube. Two other texts were written some months later. The text that follows, dated 16 January 1966, is an overall objective chronicle of events.

It was in September 1861 that the first Austrian Brothers, travelling by boat down the Danube, arrived in Romania. Between Giurgiu and Bucharest, Brother Petronius and his companions, travelling in a wagon used for transporting cattle, saw wolves for the first time. They would never have expected that one hundred years later, other wild beasts would ravage the country and condemn Romanian Brothers to forced labour during several terrible years 1950-1964.

Some may consider the following pages as rhetoric, but they have no other purpose than to confirm what happened. They are the noble songs of the first generation of Romanian Brothers. You could write on the first page of this heroic poem, changing what needs to be changed, the monumental words of the heroes of Thermoplyae, 'Traveller, if you go to Rome, tell them that we remained faithful.'

The Archbishop of Bucharest, a former student of the Brothers, still imprisoned, said to our own Brother Visitor, 'Everywhere, before and during their imprisonment, the Brothers' conduct has been irreproachable, even heroic.'

Juliu Maniu, the best-known politician of the former government of Romania, and a Greek-Catholic, died in a Brother's arms, himself also a Greek-Catholic, after the two, for six months, had recited the Rosary together every evening, and in spirit made the Way of the Cross.

At the end of 1944 the war came to an end and the Russians invaded Romania. Gradually, the Communists took charge and several Austrian Brothers left the country and returned to Vienna. The remaining Brothers, most of them Romanian, continued their educational work. They were very well respected by the people, so their schools were filled with pupils. 'Soon, the Americans will arrive and we will build our schools again', people said to one another.

Then came 1948! A new constitution that would mark an important turn in the country's history was being talked about. King Michael would be obliged to leave the country which would become a republic. All private institutions were being nationalised and our schools closed and requisitioned. As regards religious congregations, the Constitution said none too clearly: 'Religious can live in community. They are, however, forbidden to undertake any social activity or any relationship with superiors outside the country, and they are not to accept any aspirants.'

There were promises and menaces to turn the Brothers away from their vocation. The two communities in Bucharest (St Andreas and St Josef) were put together and were given refuge in the archbishop's residence, the Major Seminary, close by the cathedral. Soon the Brothers were looking for work; individual or group lessons in family homes. This state of affairs faced the Brothers with very complicated problems, but as mature and experienced men they found solutions. From morning until night without any respite, by tram, bus or on foot, in rain and snow, they went about Bucharest. After their travels, seated around tables, their conversations sounded like academic arguments because they brought ideas, impressions and news from every corner of the capital. They often spoke about the spies and informers who followed the Brothers everywhere, often introducing themselves to the Brothers to flatter them, but especially to denounce them.

In the Nuncio's Palace (the last Nuncio being a US citizen), there were three Brothers one of whom was in charge of the duplicator. This was how they distributed the texts for the cathedral ceremonies to the youth groups. The evening meetings became real demonstrations of faith. A group of students asked the Brothers to organise religion courses so they could carry out catechism classes in the different parishes of the capital. The Brothers accepted their request even though it was extremely dangerous. Young people regularly gathered with the Brothers in the evenings while others kept vigil in the street in front of the house. Different general methods of teaching were discussed, catechetical method particularly, and educational problems. Each lesson finished with a formation lesson, followed by the comments of all those who took part. Thanks be to God that these lessons were never disturbed. The young people, in their turn, gave their courses in the parishes.

The English Sisters were also obliged to close their schools, but were allowed to remain in their convent until they could be relocated in their house in the country. They had a large quantity of provisions in their convent: sugar, rice, flour, lard, oil, preserves, linen, sheets ... How could they transport all these things secretly? Our young Brothers, helped by students, succeeded in saving all this treasure. The Sisters themselves laughed when they saw the Brothers sweating, grunting and loading these heavy sacks on their shoulders. Two Franciscans, seeing what was happening, took off their habits and gave a hand. The Sisters never forgot this sight.

Then came 1950, the fatal year! The Greek-Catholic Church was violently combined with the Orthodox Church. The bishops were imprisoned and several died in prison. The priests suffered the same fate. The Nuncio had to leave the country. The three Brothers employed in the Nunciature remained imprisoned. The Nunciature itself had diplomatic immunity under the protection of the Swiss embassy in Bucharest. Prior to these events, the Brothers of the Nunciature, entrusted with this responsibility by the Nuncio himself, were able, in spite of the risks they ran, to maintain contact with the other bishops. During the night of 19 July 1950, this was the culminating point of the tragedy. A Security group surrounded the palace, broke in via a window to arrest the Brothers. During the same night, the police searched the residence in the Major Seminary and arrested three Brothers. Among all the victims, two were released only after having suffered all kinds of torture. At the time of their arrest, they were barely 30 years old; after 14 years in captivity they were ruined.

After these events, the Brothers dispersed for a while. They tried to obtain official positions, thereby entering the workforce as it was called here. This was how the Brothers obtained their cards for getting food. As they were not part of any 'union' they were first of all obliged to attend special courses with a view to obtaining at least the status of a low-ranking accountant. Being employed as a workman meant even more work: unions, courses, gatherings and meetings that took another 16 hours or so. This went on for five years. In spite of it all, the Brothers continued to meet in the Major Seminary where Brother Bonifazius, their Director and Auxiliary-Provincial, welcomed them with open arms.

1955

The Geneva Conference came with the promise of peace. A period of détente and better perspectives: the names of Eisenhower and Bulganin were heard. In Bucharest there was talk of a truce, of peace, of new happenings and new hopes. One after the other the Brothers returned to their home in the Major Seminary. The dormitories were filled and Christmas preparations went ahead as in previous times. Brothers returned again to the parishes where groups of their former students awaited them. Choirs could be heard again, sung Masses, processions and First Communions. Young people came to play ping-pong but then talked about more serious problems. Meetings began and ended with prayer and hymns. Some friends advised the Brothers to be more careful because of spies but dear Brother Bonifazius feared nothing and gave the Brothers courage.

In the parishes the Brothers resumed their former Sunday activities and young people flooded in from everywhere. Sometimes parents came as well and, seated beside their children, listened to the lessons. At Christmas time and Saint Nicholas, Christmas presents were distributed to the children. There were excursions and practices for plays. It was just like the old days. It should not be forgotten that the Brothers gained their livelihood by working in factories and offices. People asked the Brothers to organise evening dances for their children. In the Romanian capital where the majority of people were Orthodox, mixed marriages were common. Parents themselves accompanied their children to these evenings. Sometimes, an ecclesiastic was invited to give a conference on a religious topic. Benediction in the chapel was the way of ending these evenings. The Brothers, and especially Brother Bonifazius, directed these activities. The Brothers languishing in prison were not forgotten. When there was a renewal of vows, each Brother had a candle with his own name and Brother Bonifazius said the formula for those who were absent. At table, on solemn occasions, a place was set with the name of the absent person. Everyone present had to say: 'You too may find yourself one day among the absent.'

During the summer of 1958 the Brothers were warned that the *Securitate* was spying on them. Shortly afterwards, on 15 August 1958, four Brothers were arrested and condemned to 20 years hard labour. In December of the same year, their confreres were able to be present at this 'Show Trial.' What did they think in listening to the condemnation of the four Brothers, sitting on the accused benches surrounded by soldiers armed to the teeth? Their confreres criminals? The faces of the condemned men were deformed, their voices hoarse after the torture they had endured during the preventative detention by the Securitate. What was the accusation? Excessive subversive influence exercised on Catholic youth, revolutionary activities in Catholic groups and being in the pay of the Vatican. After this diabolical justice, the many Catholic spectators knew only too well the fate of the accused: they were to spend years in the infernal Danube Delta, separated from the world, enslaved, so to say, and enduring the most dreadful sufferings.

The number of Brothers who were free diminished. Calm Brother Bonifazius, however, exercised a strong influence on his Brothers. The Brothers continued to go into the parishes on Sundays as usual to teach catechism. In the spring of 1959, the police came unexpectedly among the Brothers, told them to bring with them only one small bag, because in two hours they would be leaving. This was how all the Brothers were confined in villages, or in groups of three, and had for the next five years to gain their livelihood in agricultural work, living in abandoned huts and unable to leave the locality where they were.

1964

There was a general amnesty for all political prisoners in Romania. One after another, the Brothers appeared, thin, in rags, first of all those under house arrest, then the old forced labourers. Their meeting with one another was warm-hearted but brief. They could not stay in Bucharest but each had to return to where he came from.

What was the balance sheet? For 14 years, ten Romanian Brothers totalled 70 years of prison and forced labour in uranium mines and the Danube Delta. The total sum of those detained adds up to 120 years of prison.

It was the memory of the Mother House of their District, *Marienheim* in Vienna, which was a great source of consolation for the Romanian Brothers. Brother Liebhard Maria, the Provincial, ran great risks to come by car to visit practically all the Brothers, bringing them material and spiritual comfort.

It was in this way that the Brothers lived. Dispersed around the country they gained their livelihood carrying out the worst kind of work, sick and enduring cold and want. From time to time, the police would visit them to see if they were married, because for the *Securitate*, this was the only proof that they had left the religious state.

The heroic example of the Brothers will be a guiding lamp for the Catholics in Bucharest, and the young people will never forget the sacrifices of their former teachers.

These men of mature age, but still young, educated and cultured, have struggled for almost 20 years in spite of misunderstanding and death for their vocation and they demonstrated to young people, even in the most difficult circumstances, the path that leads to Our Lord.

Many Christians of the early Church won their salvation in a few minutes. Nowadays, Christians need almost to be buried alive to win eternal life. Any further comment would be superfluous.

2. Brother Dominic's Interrogation

(From *Eine Fahrt ins Blaue*, A Journey into the Blue, pp. 7-8, written in February 1966.)

Brother Dominic's narrative tells of being kept in the notorious Uranus Centre in Bucharest, having a list made of everything in his satchel, being forced always to wear metal spectacles that revealed nothing while he was being moved, led by the arm and finally having the spectacles taken off to find himself facing a well-dressed young man in ordinary clothes, smiling sarcastically at him while the following conversation took place.

Sit down. How are you, Brother Dominic? What's the news from Timisch? [where he had just been arrested. Ed] *How's that old fox, Bonifazius getting on? He also needs to take some friendly advice. You'll see just where this old billygoat has led you. Brother Dominic, take a look at this collection here. Here are photocopies of all the correspondence with Vienna and Uncle Steinberg.*[16] *Brother Dominic, why are you following that old bandit, Bonifazius? He led you astray, as he did with your ten companions. You had a room in the city and a well-paid good job in a factory. Why did you return to that robbers' hideout in the cathedral? Ah, so Rome was paying you a better salary, eh? The devil led you astray. Now, you must really pay for your mistake.*

Now my interviewer and judge began to shout and address me informally.[17] *Please don't forget! You're not here with your grandmother nor in the Vatican* (and here he smashed his fist on the desk), *nor with any devil who can save you, but in the hands of the Romanian Security Police. We've been tracking you as an old stubborn criminal, as a companion of bandits, and you must be tried.*

You have time: days, months, a whole year. Think now, Brother Dominic, of the criminals and all the swindlers among your Order's colleagues. Don't forget that we've known all this for a long time. For years we've been observing you and this collection contains everything. Look at these photos here. Do you know him? So think about it!

He printed a sheet and then another from the agent who arrested me, took one sheet and laid it on the desk, the orders for my imprisonment.

Through the open window there was a fresh breeze blowing. In the neighbourhood could be heard the sounds of happy chil-

---

[16] Probably he meant to say 'Starribacher', the name used for Brother Fridolin, the Provincial in Vienna.

[17] That is, to use the familiar single form of address as between family and friends.

dren, perhaps in a free time at school. Swallows were twittering outside the window, on the dusty panes of glass bees were climbing and on the window ledge there were flowers growing. There came the scent of ripe apricots from the garden and the smell of freshly-cut grass. Outside, life was going on as usual.

My interviewing judge signed this piece of paper he had brought. In this way was the final act of my captivity sealed. I was in 'safe' hands. On the walls of the office in golden letters there stood:

We are building a new, free, correct world and we are making new better people. Long live the Romanian Peoples' Republic! Long live the glorious Soviet army!

Well, then, in God's name! So it had begun. There followed an entire year of this horror story in the cellars of the 'Uranus', of fiery contests with my interrogating judge many nights long. Twice the barefaced lies of my faults became an artistic presentation. On a cold December day there came the court 'show trial', with especially invited members of the public. By this opportunity I saw my fellow Brothers once again at the same time as they saw me, as they were kept in separate quarters. They, like me, were in handcuffs. Their faces were lined, their appearances distorted. I could hardly recognise them. This dreary scene lasted for a whole day, from morning until night. And the sentence? Twenty years hard labour.

3. Four extracts from *Krahen und Pelikane*

Brother Dominic's first text, Krahen und Pelikane *(Crows and Pelicans) is a typewritten document of about 7000 words, written at Christmas 1965, some month after his release and arrival in Vienna. It is not so much a narrative as a series of quite vivid memories that recall the forced labour on the Danube, different moments of the train journey of the prisoners to the Danube and of certain events there. The text, which begins with a reference to Eminescu's poem 'Reverdere' – 'the Danube always flowing on' – is, at times, highly poetic as he reflects that it is the 'Mother Danube' that flows thousands of kilometres to nourish and give life to its people. The first text that follows is his almost mystical recollection as he sees his reflection in the Danube, and recalling the writings of the exiled Roman poet Ovid, considers how he too has come to gain strength and support from contemplating the Danube ...*

As I with hundreds of other sad people first knelt beside the Danube, just like Gideon in the Bible with no cup to slake my thirst, a Professor near me said, 'Two thousand years ago the exiled Roman writer Ovid perhaps did as we do on this very spot.' Just as Ovid sang of the marshy 'Ausonien', so too very often did I kneel before the Danube. When there was no wind and there was a glow from the pebbles in the clear water, then my Danube 'flask' was transformed into a clear mirror into which I could smile and in a mocking way address myself:

You are a condemned person, you are a bandit of the tenth brigade[18] condemned for 20 years in this swamp. You were supposed to be a teacher, you showman, just like a wretched dog with your big hungry eyes and your drooping ears. You, with your baggy zebra-striped clothes, dressed again in your filthy prison clothes. You have no shirt and under your half-opened smock you can twice count your ribs and your shrunken stomach. Yes, my dear bandit, when you have no more roots, come to the water where Oros von Stoenesti lies,[19] where like so many others, you've been driven like a slave. Like every other prisoner, I grieved also many a long year yet always felt support. Ever since I came to 'Mother Danube' I have always been soothed

---

[18] His work group.
[19] One of the villages beside the river where the dam was built.

and, taking her as an example, my troubles have been taken away. I've never lost my way, nor have I stood still, I've never lost my direction or what I believe in. Following your example, I have in freedom gained courage. Heaven is not yet, but I've kept going, preserved my health and have cheerfully learned how to carry my cross' (page 2).

Extract 2

The next few pages describe the train journey from Gherla[20] *on 8 October, 50 men crowded into a completely dark compartment intended for carrying animals, with a water bucket and a toilet bucket in the corner, the little food they had been given eaten at once, with no knowledge of where they were going or how long the journey might take.*

II. **The notorious Gherla in Siebenburgen** is neither the first nor the last station if someone is moving from one prison to another. The person arriving in Gherla is already an old prisoner and knows the rules of the banished: eating to stay alive, admitting to nothing, outwitting guards, always remaining quite normal, never trusting newcomers. His ear listens to the footsteps of the guard, his eye quickly sees shadows as through a magnifying glass. He knows that from a broom he can get a sharp piece of wood and make a needle, from his shirt he can take a thread and mend his sock, he can create a frame and with wool he can make a stocking. With his brain so quickly alert, he can quickly get a firm hidden grip on everything – and become the 25th person with no body, no expression. He is as hard as stone, as cunning as a weasel, and as quiet as a mouse. He loves mice and flies as special friends; he speaks and converses with them.

---

[20] The most notorious prison in Romania in which the Lutheran Pastor Richard Wurmbrand, founder of The Voice of Martyrs, was imprisoned.

All of this sounds idyllic, romantic and peaceful. But what lies in and behind all this are hunger and thirst. From time to time there come movement, milling crowds, crashing about in the heart of this 'magic castle'. Strong actions merit punishments and often you hear loud shrieks, shrill rhythmic rolling sounds coming ever closer. Soon you hear in the cell next door the name of some 'sacrifice', and it's payday. Then everything is still again. Dirty memories creep into the poor devil like snakes: arrest, being led, lashings, terrible blows, dislocation of limbs, teeth knocked out. Feverish nerves make the hands shake, the heart leaps into the throat, you fall into a cold sweat and your stomach cramps. So many people received two, three, four or more beatings with stoic defiance. But with time, with years, there was no more time wasted in yearnings. The will smoulders and goes out; a man becomes small and as sensitive as a child, frail like a mayfly. Only shrewdness remains; cunning is the weapon of the weak.

III. **Gherla in the 4th month, on 8 October**. Late in the evening the door of our overcrowded assembly room was suddenly thrown open and the heartless 'OUT' rang through the very marrow of our bones. In the long, smelly, half-dark corridor there were armed soldiers. A sergeant called out numbers and then our names and birthdays were called out. Then once the queue was seated, each prisoner received a loaf of bread and some rancid bacon as rations for three days. Many ignored the directions and, in spite of the prohibition, ate with feverish hands what they had received. It was so long since we had seen bread. Then we were driven in a truck through the dark sleeping town. Our time in Gherla the capital was over.

Through clouds of coal smoke behind the railway station we saw two dark wagons like spectres in the night. The truck backed up against a black monster, the tailgate went down and we clambered over the bridge into the animal compartment. Once we were all inside the door of the wagon was closed. Bolts and padlocks were made secure and we were locked inside. A sergeant knocked on the outside wooden partition and called out in a low voice:

'Listen carefully inside. You have food for three days. In one corner there's drinking water and in the other there's water for relieving yourselves.'

Well, now, 50 men in a small livestock wagon, completely dark, the tiny windows covered with metal ... Slowly and carefully we lay down together, crushed together like sardines. We ate, jammed together, laughed, swore, prayed. As the freight train began to move, many made the Orthodox sign of the cross. Nobody saw this but you felt it from the movement of the elbows.

'Who knows where we're going?' asked someone. Many thought it was the Danube swampland; others, pessimists or for a laugh, said briefly, 'To Siberia, where we'll at least have movement and fresh air.'

'You will soon enough have your wish for fresh air. Don't you understand just how many people have for years been building a canal in the Danube Delta. Awaiting you are hunger, slave labour and broken bones. As far as I'm concerned, I'd prefer to stay in a cell.' It was the voice of a Major who had been two years in a Russian concentration camp.

In another corner, someone asked someone for 'water' and rightly so. The floor was wet over the sitting area. From now on everything was sodden. The wagon swayed and rattled like a windmill. The water underfoot sloshed about over the brim. Very soon the toilet bucket spilled over and flowed the same way. Where will all this end?

Three days and three nights in the same overflowing, dark

wagon, without any room for movement; hours with long painful minutes.

The train stopped often, sometimes for hours at a time, with another sound of rattling wagons and when the resounding noise was heard, then life came into this sweating mass of flesh. Those who were sleeping woke up; the nerves remained on edge. Somewhere in a corner sat two humorous Carpathian shepherds who continually tried out their wit. The taller of them was dark Ion, with his humorous stories and happy songs with which he entertained us.

'I won't have any rest until I find a hole so that I can see outside. I must know where we are.' After a while he sat up strongly:

'Up there is a plank that might be useful. I'll probe at it with my finger and see if I can drag off what it is blocking.' The train was again moving and everything in the compartment was still. Only the swarthy Ion growled in his corner:

'Mike, stand up. I'm so restless. I must see something. I'll climb on your shoulders because I've found a hole.' Shortly afterwards you could hear the two grunting and whispering and then came the welcome cry: 'Children, I can see outside. There are mountains, rings of mountains, marvellous hills, sheep, freedom. Children, outside there is freedom and we're fouled up here. Everywhere there are beech trees, all over the place, white beech trees. Now there are houses and I can see a signpost 'Ghimesch-Palanka', there it is, Ghimesch, Ghimesch.

Life came back to people. We had crossed the Carpathians of which Ghimesch is a saddle, a well-known pass between Transylvania and Moldova.

The train came to a stop. A hard sound came from outside on the wood. It rang like a hammer blow. Ion uttered a terrible curse. 'Now that so-and-so has closed up my spy hole.'

The new splendour was gone. Where are we still going to? Right down or left up or straight on?

We were in an animal wagon with soaking floorboards where sticky sweat and toilet moisture were mixed and each filthy, dirty washbundle was sopping wet. Now it was over 50 hours. A terrible apathy. You can only guess at the aching bones and the foul entrails. Always there was that relentless sound of the wheels. Hunger and lack of air had the poor devils drugged; they did not sleep, they did not wake; they didn't want anything.

IV. **It was 11 October**. The train came to a stop. Everyone realised that there was nothing more. Steps could be heard outside and shouts, and then a harsh sound of metal scraping and the frozen wagon door was opened. A sharp cold wind like a knife in the lungs followed and then a blinding light. We didn't even hear the universal cry of 'Out' but the heads of officers holding their noses appeared in the doorway. None of them knew anything. In their eyes, these arrivals were unreliable, bursting with curiosity, disgusting, something to be uneasy about. Then the officers moved on, probably onto the next wagon. The first man near the door rushed out, rolled over and writhed on the ground. Many vomited. I went into terrible convulsions in my stomach and lower abdomen as the cold, the fresh air and the unaccustomed all took their effect.

Around us stood many armed soldiers, all of them restless, with nosy wolfhounds. The soldiers were struck dumb when we fell out of the clouds. What was going on in their heads? A cloudy, sad-looking autumn day, a white lake – the Danube like a never-ending enormous tile. Could this be the uncreated heart-blood of European culture, the Danube, discreet and flowing here?

On the renowned Danube shore, southwards from the river port of Braila, there stood eight hundred prisoners in a long· column, surrounded by soldiers. Hot tea and soaked maize bread had been brought to the people. We could talk and laugh quietly. On the horizon could be seen a second smaller column of prisoners in their zebra-striped clothing with bundles of washing under their arms. Our train was closed up. Officers and sergeants came in front of us and began to inspect us and give us advice. Someone in charge gave us a short talk of which I understood nothing. Then the group surrounding us opened up slowly and we came with small steps to the Danube. In the middle of the stream there was a motor boat filled with soldiers, probably to prevent anyone springing into the water.

Into the Danube went a thousand men knee-deep. We had to drink and wash our faces. The water was lukewarm but a great deal warmer than the raw, cold wind. Mother Danube was giving her children something to drink. The die was cast (pages 2-7).

Extract three

This third extract is another of the writer's vivid memories of a particular moment in the six years spent in forced labour on the Danube.

I myself began to believe as I looked back at my portrait that I had a good Guardian Angel. I was smaller than most, and didn't suffer as much from hunger. My white hair, my pale Gandhi look, gave me a somewhat blessed appearance. I recall one evening when the sergeant's hand was on my shoulder to hurry me up, when I heard another guard whisper, 'Leave him alone, he looks just like my father' (pages 13-14).

Extract four

In this section towards the end of his text, Brother Dominic seems to recall the end of a working day and contrasts the freedom of the birds with that of the long line of sad prisoners being escorted back to their confinement.

It is evening. The ever watchful soldiers are resting, the idle wolfhounds doze near the machine gun posts, the golden sun dips below the darkening hills beyond the Danube.

'Listen!' A joyful prolonged cry from hundreds of throats rings out along the Dam. After an hour, there will come warm maize-bread and soft palliasses. Dogs bark, soldiers call out and warn us to line up. When this is done, it's 'forward march.'

At the same time so many water birds are also on the way home, wild geese in triangular formation towards the west, pelicans in white lines towards the east, nimble ducks buzz like arrows through the air, herons with stylish-shaped necks, swans also, all three birds with long outstretched necks, all going home. Far above us fly these happy free birds of the Danube, this swamp in all its uncreated abundance for thousands, for millions of years this same peaceful picture. Below them is a water paradise.

The sun has set and the long train of prisoners is marching. Never far away smoulders the half burning same dead pain as the poorest of men under heaven suffer. Endless rows of barbed wire; then the gate like the enormous maw of a dragon; hot, hot maize-bread; then the thought of a pleasant shower from head to toe; then the palliasse.

In the vast dormitory are 100 double bunks for 200 people. Everything is quiet. Now an owl hoots over the rotten reed-thatched roof. Then it is quiet again. Gong tones ring around the prisoners' fence, the signals of the sentries who have to report hourly. Then quiet once more. Near me a Romanian signs himself with three great crosses. From one corner comes the sigh of someone dreaming, 'Mama' (pages 16-17).

CHAPTER SIX

In Romania: A Long Night that Lasted 42 Years

Brother Tiberiù's text, first written in August 1991 after the collapse of the Ceauşescu regime, is a graphic, still angry account of events that took place over 40 years previously. Because he continually questioned his guards about his imprisonment, he seems to have been given special attention and never left without supervision or without having to report once a week to the Securitate.

Brother Tiberiù's Personal Account

My way of the cross began on 2 August 1948. It was the last day of our annual retreat. The Directors of the three Catholic schools run by the Brothers in Bucharest were summoned to appear by the Romanian Communist authorities who were in power. They were informed that the Communist government intended to nationalise private (free) schools. The Brothers were told to hand over the keys of the schools immediately. Within an hour we found ourselves thrown out into the street. We had been allowed to take only our personal effects like linen, shoes, etc. All the rest – library books, beds, cupboards, etc. – had to be left in the school. We were told also that we could not live as a community and that we would be employed as teachers. If this did not materialise we would have to survive as best we might.

The authorities decreed we had to live in a small flat on the second floor of the Roman Catholic bishop's house. This decree applied only to religious who worked in schools. The Jesuits and Franciscans, who were priests, were not included, but they had to abandon their religious habit and they went into the parishes. Each of us had to indicate his agreement or disagreement [about staying or leaving. Ed.] in writing.

Only the Brothers of the Christian Schools were affected by this decree. The two Brothers' communities merged into one under the leadership of the Director and Auxiliary-Visitor, Brother Bonifazius Sattmann. There were about 20 of us.

At 24, I was one of the youngest. I had taught for only three years at St Joseph's school. I did not hesitate a moment as to what I should do. I realised that my place had to be among the Brothers and with them. Also I was convinced that the situation would not last a long time. There were two Brothers younger than myself. Unfortunately, both left later for various reasons. Subsequently they regretted their decision, even though our life was not easy. By applying pressure and making promises, the Communist authorities tried to make us abandon religious life. They failed.

Brother Boniface (Bonifazius) was bursar and superior at a difficult time. His trust in Providence impressed us all and gave us courage. None of us was either faint-hearted or cowed, even if this was not always easy. He was the father, the leader and everybody's friend despite his deafness. He prayed a lot precisely because he was deaf. After the grace of God, it was to him that we owed our community life. He was the superior that Providence had prepared for us and given us for those troubled times.

It was not long before the first difficulties arose. Our meagre resources were exhausted. To survive, the Brothers had to give private lessons. The parents wanted this. This was my work for five years. It was a new form of apostolate. Through these private lessons we continued to exercise a religious influence. It was more important than ever.

Soon we began to teach catechism in the parishes. For two years we encountered no problems. It was the calm before the storm. The first storm broke out in 1950. Five Brothers were arrested. Two of them who had worked in the Nunciature were tried in court and sent to prison for 16 years. The two others were condemned without a proper trial to two years' hard labour.

For safety's sake, some of the Brothers were lodged with former students. There followed a period of calm: the great Moloch was sated with his offerings ...

After the Helsinki Conference, it looked as if the clouds would clear up. The Brothers returned to their flat and restarted their catechism classes in five parishes where every Sunday some 300 Catholics would gather. This was not to the liking of the Communist authorities. They would say to their colleagues: 'You can't manage to organise Communist youth meetings, and yet this handful of religious teachers fills its hall every Sunday.' Former students and friends warned the Brothers that trouble was brewing. Brother Boniface remained calm and continued to inspire his Brothers to be faithful and trust in God.

For two years we had taught religion surrounded by spies. We knew who they were and they knew who we were. They were waiting for orders to act. The orders arrived on 21 August 1958: four Brothers were arrested and with them three former students who had recruited other students. After three months of investigation, painful interrogation and even torture, the sentences were handed down on December 17th 1958: 90 years in prison. The two older Brothers were each given 20 years, the three others 15 years each, and the two youngest each got 10 years.

And their crime? They had taught religion to young people. This is the reason given in the text of sentence M 1252-58. I enclose a copy in French and in Italian. What was their justification for sentencing people to 10, 15 or 20 years in prison? They say they belong to supposedly the most humane form of society in the world. How can anybody in his right mind understand their behaviour? And these Communists, who condemned people for such 'crimes' to the harshest prisons that existed, were not ashamed to put it all down in writing. What is your reaction, you westerners, to such a travesty of justice? And you, Communists of the western world, what do you think of your universal brotherhood and justice now? The eastern block alliance!

And so our troubles began again. There were 110 of us in a room measuring 11 metres by 10. There was one window, but it was boarded up with planks nailed down on the outside to prevent the prisoners from looking out. In one corner, to attract the rats, there were four buckets (there was no lavatory). The buckets were free once or twice a day. No one could stay close to the windows: it was absolutely forbidden.

We slept on the bare concrete floor, not that we could lie on our backs since there was not enough room; we had to lie on our sides, pressed together like sardines. Often and most of the time, the most recent arrivals in the room would have to sleep sitting on the buckets that served as lavatories.

Soon, our bodies were one big sore. There was no water. Each person was allowed half a litre of water per day. There was no soap. Here and there some little scraps of soap. No toilet paper. Half an hour exercise in a yard about 30 metres square, wide spaces between persons, so you could not speak to neighbours, or even see them really. No one was allowed to speak. A warder (a policeman) supervised.

During the daytime no one was allowed to have a rest in bed, except those who were sick and had the doctor's permission. You were not allowed to give talks nor listen to them; you could not study foreign languages nor teach them. We did not have the means to write; there was no paper, no pencils, not even a needle. Everything was strictly forbidden. Anyone caught infringing these laws was put into solitary confinement for three to five days. In the solitary confinement cell, it was forbidden to sit between 5.00 am and 10.00 pm. You were fed only twice a day and you were given only 100 grams of bread and half a litre of salty water.

At this point the reader will perhaps say I am mistaken, or I am exaggerating. Not at all, there is no mistake. I recommend he reads Solzhenitsyn's book *Gulag Archipelago*. He does not deceive. He does not exaggerate. In his book you will find a complete catalogue of the unimaginable inhuman cruelties inflicted by these people.

After a year of such treatment, prisoners were asked if they wanted to work. Of course, all those that were able to move replied in the affirmative. And so, in August 1959, we were loaded into cattle wagons, each having the same lavatory arrangements already mentioned. After two days and a night we set off for an unknown destination. As the wagons were open we were able to see that we were being taken to the region called *Grosseinsel du Danube*, in the vicinity of Braila. There we had to build an embankment 17 metres high and 35 kilometres long as a barrier against the turbulent waters of the Danube. We were lodged in two huts. There were about 800 of us. Conditions were worse than primitive. The greatest problem was the water. A litre of water to mix with a sort of coffee, half water half mud, and you had to wait as long as up to 3.00 am to get it.

The consequences were not long in making themselves felt. From the tenth day onwards, August 17th, we suffered from dysentery. It was very dangerous. There was no doctor. I had only ten Talasol tablets. For seven days I could not eat or drink anything. Really nothing. I was dying. I had suffered from it in prison and now I had it for the second time.

It is perhaps difficult to believe that I am saying nothing but the truth. In the space of two weeks I had become a skeleton. It was also the first time that I saw a man die. It made a great impression on me. His condition had not seemed any worse than mine. I, however, had not lost all hope. It was very difficult at the beginning and it continued to be so for a long time. I had to return to work but I was so weak that I could hardly walk. Many people died at this time.

In the month of November I had to return to work on the embankment. We had to build it with picks and shovels. It was very difficult. Often we thought of the Egyptians building the pyramids. Was it as exhausting as this? Let's not exaggerate, some will think …

After two years we were sent out to work in the fields. It was less exhausting. During the course of 1961, we were sent to Luciu Giurgen. To drink, we fetched water from the Danube and boiled it. This did not last long. Once again we fell ill. This time it was typhus (typhoid fever). In November I fell ill too. I was singled out to be examined by a commission of civilian doctors. I was in danger of dying and so they moved me to a hospital in Constanta. It was the second time I found myself at death's door. Here we were well cared for. After three weeks, the danger had passed and we were able to return to the camp and take up some other form of work. This was something almost unheard of. On my way back I spent a never-to-be-forgotten Christmas night in a hovel in company with other vermin like myself and hundreds or thousands of mice, all curious to know what I was looking for and why I had come there to disturb their peace and quiet. It was impossible to sleep under such circumstances.

In autumn 1962, I was taken back to the well-known prison at Gherla. Because of my illness, I had now been a germ carrier for 15 years and was considered to be a source of danger for the civilian inhabitants of this island. No one was concerned about the prisoners even when they fell ill.

At Gherla I worked for two years in a furniture factory, making tables. I was better off materially. Those who fulfilled their 'norms' were given a postcard and were able to write home asking for a parcel weighing no more than five kilos and containing food and 400 cigarettes. I wrote only once, although I became a good maker of tables.

In spring 1964 we were allowed for the first time in five and a half years to read a book. We were permitted also to read the party newspaper which told of the successes of the people under the leadership of the Romanian Communist party. They wanted to prepare us slowly for our liberation which was approaching.

I think it was April when they told us we would be freed, but not all at the same time. This was the first time they kept their word: the first prisoners were released in April and I had to wait for my turn till 1 August 1964.

As I had had no news of the Brothers for six years I was taken first to my family. They lived relatively close, some 110 kilometres away and 50 kilometres from Bucharest. I had no money and I wanted to know if my mother was still alive, because she was 77 years old and had had a heart attack in spring 1958, and in the autumn of that year I had been sent to prison. For a long time I had thought she was dead. I was very attached to my mother as she had been largely responsible for my vocation to the Brothers.

My meeting with her was very moving both for her and for me. I cannot bring myself to describe that moment. Even after so many years it would still be difficult. For a long time she wept in my arms, repeating over and over again 'my dear child, my dear child'. And I wept with her. Everyone in the house did as we did. We all wept – for joy.

I remained four days at my mother's house. I very much wanted to go back to the Brothers in Bucharest. I was the last one to arrive, all the others were already there. It was a joyful but rather short meeting. We could not remain in Bucharest. We could not form a community. In the eyes of the Communists we were dangerous people. We had to leave Bucharest without delay. Three Brothers were able to stay in Bucharest because they had relatives there; the others had to return to the place of their origin.

And so the second stage of our sentence began. This was a much longer period to endure even if its difficulties did not match those of prison, which were very harsh and which I shall never forget. It was a period that lasted 25 years. The Communists always thought of us as lepers and a danger to the State. The people, however, thought differently about us. They loved and respected us. One day, an officer of the *Securitate* said to me: 'What is dangerous for us is simply your name of Brothers of the Christian Schools.'

I had to keep alive somehow and so I went to the authorities to ask for work. They replied: 'For someone like you the only work we've got is down the mines.' I then had recourse to my friends. There were some understanding people among them. After four months I found work as a librarian. The salary was small but was enough to keep body and soul together. I was lucky also to be helped by some relatives who lived locally. They gave me the means to survive. They had no money. I received a lot of help from five Hungarian Brothers from Satu Mare. They had had the good fortune to be able to remain together.

They lived a long way from Bucharest, some 700 kilometres away, on the border with Hungary. They were all old. Every two months I would visit them to soak up a little community spirit. They always showed great friendship and kindness to me. Although they are all dead now, I wish to say to them how grateful I am for all the brotherly love they showed me.

Accommodation posed a great problem. I could not find any. Finally one of my relatives took pity on me. He had a new house but only one room was in a fit state to live in. The other rooms had neither windows nor doors. There were four young children. And so for three months I had to share this single room with them. I had to make the best of it; there was no alternative. Every morning, the master of the house would greet us with 'Live Jesus in our hearts!' for he had been a junior novice with us for two years. Since then he has become a priest of the Greek Catholic rite. In February I was able to sleep alone. During the day, I spent most of my time with the children, because there was not enough wood to heat two rooms. I helped the children to fetch wood. I remained for three and a half years with this family, and then in 1968 I found a room in a concrete bunker measuring four metres by two and a half metres.

At the beginning, I was always under close supervision. They always knew where I was. I was not yet able to establish contact with the Brothers who had lived with me in Bucharest. This became possible only two years later when supervision was relaxed.

In autumn 1965 Brother Liebhard from Vienna came to see me. He knew all the Romanian Brothers because he had been a

teacher in Romania before 1948. He did not come empty-hand-
ed. The same thing had happened in May 1964, but I was still in
prison at the time. The visit of the Brothers from Austria was a
great source of encouragement for us. We felt that we were not
forgotten or abandoned. We were made to feel that the great
Lasallian family was a reality.

The Brother Visitor invited us to come and live in Vienna. At
that time we were relatively young, between 40 and 54 years old,
and we knew some German. Moreover, we could be given help
there. He obtained all the documents needed for us foreigners.
Austria gave us an entry visa, but the Romanian authorities refused to let us leave. And so we remained in Romania. At least
once a year, the Brother Provincial would come from Vienna
to visit us. Later, other superiors also came. The Assistant, Br
Richard, came twice; and the Brother Vicar himself, Br John
Johnston (now Superior General) came to see us.

These visits were for us an opportunity to meet fellow Brothers. We were often called in for questioning. They wanted to
know who our guests were and what they wanted. They were
frightened we were getting ourselves organised. They did not
allow us to live in community. From time to time, here and
there, they would ask us when we were going to get married.
That would have been a proof for them that we had abandoned
our vocation. Thank God, we have all persevered up to now.

With time, our links were strengthened. We met more often, either to celebrate a birthday or mark a feast. In 1970 a little
miracle occurred – it was certainly one for me. Brother Tarcisius, who had been in prison for 14 years, obtained a passport
(the first one of us to do so), and was able to visit Vienna, Rome
and Paris. It was an occasion to remember! The second time he
applied he was refused.

The days of anguish were over. Even the supervision became

discreet. But we could not teach religion. We could go to church as often and for as long as we wanted. We had daily Mass. No one forbade it. It was impossible to take up community life again and wear the religious habit. The number of Brothers diminished slowly. The Hungarian Brothers of Satu Mare all died at an advanced age. All were over 80. The last one died in 1983.

Brother Tarcisius died suddenly, 61 years old, of a heart attack on 25 November 1977. On 9 November he had celebrated his 60th birthday. His death affected us deeply. He had consistently and tirelessly fought Communism. Even in prison he had always protested vigorously when prisoners were mistreated.

In 1983, my turn arrived to obtain a passport. It was almost incredible. That same year another Brother also obtained a passport. And so I spent a month with the Brothers in Vienna. In 1987, I was allowed to go abroad again. This time it was much easier as I was a retired person. I went to Rome and was able to be present at the beatification of Brother Arnould. It had always been my dream to see Rome and the Generalate. That dream became a reality a second time in 1989, when I spent six weeks at the International Lasallian Centre in Rome.

The end of 1989 brought us new hope. At Christmas, we were able to hear Christmas carols again and, with permission, watch Mass on television. The long night of 42 years of oppression was beginning to fade. The Communist system (the government) was overthrown. We could breathe again. And we could sing a *Te Deum* in our hearts. We did not dare believe it was all true.

Unfortunately, one year later, we see that the new authorities do not seem to take religious freedom all that seriously. Religious communities are still not recognised, and convents and property have not yet been handed back. We Brothers, despite our age and our small number, have finally left the night behind.

One Brother teaches in the seminary of Alba Julia, another at that of Iasi. He is following up an aspirant who wants to become a Brother of the Christian Schools.

On the feast of Christ the King, a small community was set up at Oradea, 15 kilometres from the Hungarian border. Above all, we have been invited to take up our work again in the places where we worked before. Although we are few in number, six Brothers, two of them ill, and between 67 and 81 years of age, we are optimistic and put our trust in Providence. The 14 canonised and beatified Brothers will help us. The work of St John Baptist de La Salle in Romania cannot and must not die.

We turn to all the Brothers in the world, and ask them not to forget us and to remember us in their prayers. We will win, but not because of what we do. Our holy Brothers and the 150,000 Brothers of the Christian Schools who over the centuries have worn our habit will be with us. They will help us. We are convinced that God is helping us and when God 'is for us, who will be against us?'

(Published in *Rundbrief*, 1992, No.1, pp. 20-23, in German, and in the Institute *Bulletin*, No. 235, September 1991 (French, Spanish, English).

Translation of the Decree of the Military Tribunal of Bucharest, No. 1252

Condemnation of Rata V. Romul George (Brother Tiberiù), 17 December 1958

Today there was a public meeting to judge the case of RATA V. ROMUL GEORGE known as Tiberiù, born on 2 May 1924 in the Commune of Arduaat, District of Semcuta Mare, region of Baia

Mare, son of Vasile and Florea, a professor monk, unmarried, having no fortune, having completed military service satisfactorily, is presently in the CM [military prison] of the quarter Gh.Gh.Dej. He states that he has no previous conviction; his education shows him to be licensed in Philology and Pedagogy; his social background is that of a poor peasant; his last permanent address is in Bucharest, Nr. 19 Papov street in the Gh. Gh. Dej quarter; arrested by Bucharest Military Unit 0125/E; accused of conspiracy against the social order paragraphs of article 209, point 2, letters a.c.p., combined with the letter b on line 2 of the same article.

RATA ROMUL GEORGE known as Tiberiù has been a teacher/monk since 1945 at the Saint Joseph Secondary School in Bucharest under the patronage of the congregation known as 'Brothers of the Christian Schools'. From 1945 to 1948 he was a member of this congregation and in 1949, following the suppression and outlawing of the above so-called congregation, he had an occupation before following a course in pedagogy in a school. As according to the established rules he was no longer to live life as a monk, he took on a job. The accused, however, withdrew with other monks of the cloister in the old building of the Roman Catholic archbishop in No. 19 Papov street where he lived and continued to take part in daily activities with others, following the rules established by the congregation which has been forbidden and suppressed. In this way, he himself took part in the daily education which was carried out by the presentations of retrograde accounts and commentary on them. He also took part in meetings and spiritual exercises which were held in the building at No. 19 Papov street.

He even took part until 1958 in catechetical activities, giving lessons in religion to young pupils in the cathedral of Saint Teresa at the Belu cemetery in Bucharest. In the course of the religion lessons which he taught to the pupils and to others, he gave them a mystical and religious education in which he sought to distance his hearers from the Marxist-Leninist doctrine and to stifle them with retrograde ideas about life and the world.

In the discussions which he carried on with other monks who had been members of the congregation of the 'Brothers of the Christian Schools', in 1957-1958, he stated, speaking about events that had happened in Poland and Hungary, that the democratic regime was going to be changed and he hoped that at the same time they would regain their former privileges.

He even stated that the teaching of religion in school would be permitted again, and he and the others denigrated the way pupils in the popular democracy state schools were being prepared, affirming that in the problem of teaching, the Romanian Peoples Republic was only copying Soviet methods.

He even stated that there was more freedom in the West. He praised the science of the capitalist states in the presence of other people and he passed on news to other monks from imperialist radio stations, news which gave an unfavourable idea of the government of the Peoples Democracy.

In a unanimous vote, applying Article 209 point 2, letters a.c.p. combined with b.c.p. article 463 C.J.M. and r04 CJM, RATA ROMUL GEORGE known as Tiberiù is condemned to 15 (fifteen) years of forced labour and deprived of citizenship for ten years.

Conformable to article 25 point g on line 1 c.p., there is total confiscation of the personal fortune of all those condemned.

He is obliged to pay the State 400 (four hundred) *lei* for expenses.

The preventative detention begins on 21 August 1958

[The original document is stamped with the Military Tribunal seal.]

Bratislava, 1.12.'89

Very dear Brother Councillor,

Herewith I am sending you a short
report of the work and vicissitudes
of the Brothers of the Czechoslovak
District after World War II. I collected the necessary dates and informa-
tions as best I could. It is unfortunate
that I had no one to revue this little
work with respect to such details as
exact time and numbers. As to the facts
and events you will have to rely on my
honesty. Will perhaps some clever pen
give my poor account a better shape?
         Please, give our humble regards
to the Most Honoured Brother.
         With religious greetings and
     Best wishes for the Holy season,
              Yours obediently
                   Bro. J. Rybňský

CHAPTER SEVEN

Overview of the Czechoslovakia District in 1989

T*he handwritten letter on the facing page, by Brother Ján Rybansky, from the Archives of the Brothers of the Christian Schools, Rome, was written and addressed at his request to Brother Gerard Rummery, General Councillor in liaison with the Brothers of Eastern Europe [except Poland] from 1986 to 1993. It is the only overall account written about this period.*

[NOTE: Brother Ján's English, learned first in Dover and spoken mainly in Sri Lanka 1928-1947, is clear and simple in its expression, perhaps a little 'quaint' to contemporary ears, but the reader has no difficulty in sensing his pride in the achievements of the Brothers, and his sadness at the savage way in which these works for the poor were brought to an end.]

FSC District of Czechoslovakia after World War II

The District of Czechoslovakia reached its greatest development in the years just before the Second World War. In Bohemia the Brothers managed three important institutions: an elementary boarding school with a post-primary section at Bubenec, Prague;

a normal school [i.e., a teachers' college. Ed.] at Sv. Ján pod Skalou (St John under the Rock), near Beroun, and a home for apprentices and orphans with an elementary school in Prague, in
Salmová, known as Joanneum.

1. Praha-Bubenč

A community of eight Brothers led by Bro. Frantisek Kovár held
an elementary boarding school with a post-primary section with a
total number of about 160 pupils out of which some 50 were boarders. It was a typical Brothers' school, highly esteemed, so that many
a well-situated family thought it a boon to have their sons educated
there. An Archconfraternity of the Holy Child, centred on the famous shrine 'Jezulátko', the Little Jesus of Prague, was established
there thanks to Bro. Henry Rybansky recently come back from Sri
Lanka for a long holiday. Good Bro. Cestmír Kumpera, who died at
Moravec 25/7/1989, became the first Moderator. Soon a new spirit
of tender devotion to the Holy Child and his Immaculate Mother
animated the whole school, mindful of the alleged words of Jesus
to the Prague citizens, 'As you honour me, I will protect you.'

A course of English was opened for adults, and in a short
time more than 100 intellectuals took advantage of it, for Bro.
Henry found excellent helpers in two other 'English' Brothers.
Even an Academy was envisaged when the Communist disaster
overwhelmed the country. The school was nationalised in 1949
and the Brothers went to teach Catechism at a large school in
Praha-Smichov, not for long however, as early in 1950 all Catholic schools were taken over by the 'state' and all religious were
arrested and interned in 'concentration' monasteries.

The last community comprised: Brothers Frantisek Kovár,
Dtr, Kajetán, Cestmír, Augustín Rybánsky, Oldrich Mikula, Bohumír Nevbedel, Rehor Pozár.

Just two remarks that might serve as footnotes. Dr J. Kubicek, MP in the first Republic, once said to the writer of this report: '... daily we thank God that we came to know the Brothers and had our two boys educated at Bubenec school'. This school was the first Catholic school to be closed by the Nazis and one of the first to be seized by the Communists.

The Brothers could rise to real heroism. Occasion occurred in 1942 when a pupil of theirs, a bit of a scamp, heedless of the possible consequences, scribbled an epithet concerning Hitler. The Gestapo sought the boy and threatened all the Brothers with dire reprisals if they did not disclose the culprit to their Provincial. Bro. Arnost, pleaded with the German police, day in day out, and if thrown out by one door, he re-entered by another. In the end two Brothers were picked for the concentration camp: Bro. Ceslav Dlouhy and Bro. Matus [Matthew]. As long as they shared the horrors of the camp together, they bore their lot patiently, but on being separated, poor Bro. Matus wept as they embraced, to break one's heart. He was heard of no more. Bro. Ceslav survived and remembered the camp as a horror dream. In 1950 he was arrested again, by the Communists this time, and sent to Osek along with other religious.

Later he rendered the Sisters of Notre Dame very good services till his somewhat sudden death in 1977. He was very helpful to the District, translating Institute literature from German. Brother Ceslav was a gentle, saintly Brother. A simple tombstone in the Osek cemetery keeps memory of him.

2. Normal School at Sv. Ján pod Skalou
(St John under the Rock)

This was an important boarding school some 25 km southwest of Prague, situated in beautiful surroundings not far from the historical Karlstein. Besides ample modern buildings fully equipped for 160 future teachers, the establishment comprised a park, large gardens watered by a stream, a considerable part of the nearby forest, and the famous rock overlooking the buildings. Once a large boulder detached itself high up from the rock and, strangely enough, changed its course, hurtled down past the buildings and broke up in the park. A statue of Our Lady in the niche left by the boulder commemorates this event.

The Institution dates back to 1908 when 'The Association of St Wenceslaus' resolved to establish a four-year normal school. The Cardinal Archbishop of Prague and all the bishops of Bohemia and Moravia gave a wholehearted welcome to the project, and the Ministry for Church Affairs gave its approval under the following conditions: 1. Suitable buildings. 2. Qualified staff. 3. Adequate teaching aids.

These conditions were fulfilled and the very next year the College opened its doors to the first batch of 40 teaching candidates. In the following three years, 40 new candidates were added each year so that by 1913 all the four stages were full. The institution was handed over to the Brothers and its first director was Bro. Felix Spacek, PhD.

In June 1913 the first teachers' examination took place and the results were very good indeed. Out of 40 candidates, 39 passed the examination, 29 of them with distinction. But in 1915, war conditions did not allow the completion of the college, and the archbishop of Prague, Cardinal Lev Skrbensky, bought the whole property for his small seminary. With the money received, the Brothers acquired and adapted an old Benedictine monastery at Sv. Ján pod Skalou and transferred their normal school there.

After the World War, the school had to cope with atheistic propaganda and lack of qualified personnel, but stood its ground, regained the confidence of the public and continued to send out 40 teachers annually, and train young Brothers until it was suppressed by the Nazis in 1942. It was turned into an asylum, and the Brothers, allowed to stay in the community, took care of the patients. In 1946, the whole property was seized by the Communist party.

The Brothers that remained in the community from 1942 to 1946 were Bro. Jaromír Rob, Director, and Brothers Rehor Pozár, Benedict, Filip, Bedrich. In 1946 they joined other communities. The number of graduates from the very beginning was close to 1000. Catholic activities: Marial Sodality, Abstinence Association of Catholic teachers in the lands of 'St Wenceslaus Crown'. The school was the only Catholic normal school in the Czech-speaking countries.

3. Joanneum, Praha 2, Salmová B

Originally a Catholic home for apprentices from poor families, it was confided to the Brothers in 1912. After World War I, it became also a war orphanage with an elementary school for the orphans. These, on reaching the age of 14 and finishing their primary education, passed on to the apprentice section. Gifted boys continued their education at secondary or even high schools. Here are the approximate statistics for the period just before World War II: primary education for 60 boys, secondary schools 20 boys, high schools 10 boys, apprentices 60 to 80 boys. Apprentices learnt their respective trades with trade masters in various quarters of the city, but had their home at Joanneum for board and lodging and all their needs. There they received Catholic education, assisted at liturgical celebrations and said their common prayers in a church-like chapel with a large organ. Normally a community of eight to ten Brothers with Bro.

Stepan as a long standing Director devoted themselves to this establishment. During the war, part of the personnel of the General Hospital had to be accommodated with night lodgings and this arrangement continued even after the war.

In 1946, the elementary day school of Bubenec was transferred to Joanneum where it remained until 1948 when all Catholic institutions were taken over by the State. Joanneum was the usual residence of Brother Visitor and offered ready and generous hospitality to Brothers and priests passing through Prague.

Only two Czech Brothers are still living on 10/9/1989. Bro. Bohumír (Karel Nevedel, born 19/1/1908) and Bro. Josef Pozár (17/3/1915). Many of those who have gone to God have their graves either in the Bubenec cemetery or at Moravec.

FSC Brothers in Slovakia

1, Urmín (now Mojmírovce)

The first schools of the Brothers in Slovakia were opened or taken over at about the same time as those in Prague and thanks to a similar organisation promoting Catholic schools. The chairman of the organisation, Dr Karol Tóth, District Health Officer, prayed Bro. Cosmas, Visitor of Vienna District, to send Brothers to Urmín, a large village south of Nitra. These Brothers were sent in 1899 to take over an elementary school in Urmín. The school prospered and soon a post-primary section was added for older boys. Their ever increasing numbers made it possible to introduce various activities that made the school both popular and effective: healthy sports and games, stage acting, singing in choir, and use of the public library managed and enlarged by the Brothers. To crown all, a Marial Sodality was formed for the bigger boys. Thanks to it many a young man heard the call to a higher vocation and sought admission to the seminary or the Brothers' juniorate at Bojná.

In 1931, a complex of new buildings, Brothers' quarters included, was put up and solemnly blessed by the bishop of Trnava, Dr Paul Jantausch.

A lower-secondary school was opened in 1946. Three years later a quiet celebration of the 50th anniversary of the Brothers' arrival at Urmín took place, but the Brothers felt uneasy. Communists had seized all power and acted as they pleased; a brutal, vulgar lot.

On 3 May 1950 at midnight, secret police arrested the little Urmín community: Brothers Ambroz Kostany, Director, Bernardin Elías and Alfons Bezák. They took them to Mocenok/ Sladeckovce to join other Brothers arrested there. The school shared the lot of 'nationalised' schools elsewhere.

2. Bojná

Thanks to great efforts of Dr Karol Tóth and the parish priest of Bojná, a second community of Brothers was established at Bojná, a considerable village some eight km north-west of Topolcany. At their earnest request, Bro. Cosmas sent four Brothers from Vienna with old Bro. Adolf as Director. The beginnings were hard indeed. The Brothers lacked practically everything, and the house they were to live in was an old dilapidated monastery that had served the military for retired soldiers,

After essential repairs and adaptations, they moved in with their new school and opened classes in September 1899. The school did well and a post-primary section for boarders was set up when well-to-do people sought good education for their hard-to-manage sons. They were not disappointed, and the boarding school grew. New grounds were acquired for playing fields, vegetable and fruit gardens, and even a small vineyard with a hive in it. As Bojná had no electricity, acetylene light was installed, a bakery built, and strong Bro. Bertalán serviced both. Arable land was bought for farming to provide grain, vegetables and milk for the boarders and the community. Bro. Baláz, the infirmarian, ran the farming and with the years became known far and wide as Bro. Doctor-Farmer. The garden was embellished with a pretty Lourdes grotto at the north-eastern corner and a large bronze statue of St De La Salle at the southern end.

Bojná, with its healthy surroundings, seemed ideal for houses of formation. Both novitiate and juniorate were established in 1920 and numbered eight novices and ten juniors to start with. But in 1928 the novitiate was transferred to Mocenok. The last novice master was Bro. Albert Horák, capable and hard-working even in his eighties. The juniorate was constituted a separate community in 1947 with Brother Jaroslav Rybánsky as director helped by Bro. Tibor. The juniors numbered 32.

The boarding school, a lower-secondary school, continued to prosper during the war and after it. The number of boarders rose to 120, and the day scholars, boys and girls after the war, to about as many. Modernised, it might have become an important education centre for West Slovakia, had not the Communist disaster overwhelmed the country. Commission after commission came to assure the Brothers that 'they had nothing to fear.' Then came the night of 3 May 1950. The secret police and militia broke into the house at midnight, gave the Brothers a few minutes to pack the most necessary personal things and get into a covered bus which was to take them nobody knew where. It was to Mocenok, where their confreres, lined up against the walls, 'greeted' them in absolute silence.

The school was supposed to continue with reinforced lay staff, but the frightened juniors and boarders ran away in spite of militia guards. Then the whole establishment was closed to the public.

Strange activities in the Brothers' rooms roused the curiosity of the Bojna people, and when they ceased, the Brothers in Mocenok [i.e., already imprisoned] had to line up day after day and 'confess' that they had pornography in their rooms. But the lining up ceased all of a sudden. 'What has happened?' asked the annoyed Brothers of one another. The answer came from Bojná. Obscene paintings had been hung in their rooms in Bojná and then tentatively shown to people who indignantly told the evil-doers what they thought of them, for they had seen the Brothers' rooms many times. The Brothers were spared the abominable vilification dealt to the Franciscans before.

The following Brothers were in Bojná community in May 1950: Bro. Kasián Marcin, Director; Emerich Hanuska, teacher; Tomás Jombík; Fabián Marko; Gustav, Prefect; Valér Urvinitka; Baláz, Infirmarian and Econome; Kristo Kácer, gardener; Tibor, teacher; Efrem, seriously ill; Jaronym Hanuska, School Director.

Brothers from suppressed communities: Bros Dezider Demeter; Vincent Fatransky (later a priest); Ondrej Obrobiniak; Anselm Uherík; Zdenlko Halcín.

Here I venture a critical note on the Bojná establishment. At one time the Brothers gave up the elementary school to lay direction. This was a major mistake which alienated them from the common people who thought themselves looked down upon. Another fault was to give up teaching Catechism in favour of the parish priest and under his pressure. To say the least of it, he could not cope with the work.

3. Močenok/Sladeckovce

The bishop of Nitra, Dr Karol Kmetko, came to know the Brothers and their methods in his travels abroad and wanted to have them in his diocese. In 1928 he offered them a large mansion with an extensive park in Močenok for their novitiate. That was a great favour which the Brothers readily and gratefully accepted. That same year they transferred their novitiate and, in gratitude to their distinguished benefactor, took over the local elementary school. With the munificent help of the bishop (later archbishop), the school was renovated and enlarged into a seven-year school with a branch at Králová, and a lower secondary section. It boasted a well-equipped gymnasium hall, a permanent stage, a teachers' room and cabinets for teaching aids and collections. The local public library, too, was enlarged and handed over to the Brothers' management. His Lordship was very pleased and personally opened the renovated school after solemnly blessing it in 1938.

All these advantages greatly contributed to an all-round education of the 500 odd pupils. Old boys kept in touch with their Alma Mater through well-organised sports and games, the rich library put at their disposal and the spiritual groups established in the school. Quite a number of young men sought admission to our juniorate in Bojná or the minor seminary.

When the normal school at Spisská Kapitula was suppressed, the Brothers' scholasticate found a suitable refuge in the Močenok house. In 1950 it housed the following groups:

1. The novitiate with six novices; Master of Novices Bro. Albert Horák.

2. School community with eight Brothers: Bro. Izidor Hlavác as Director; Bro. Hyacint as Sub-Director; Bro. Ladislav Dragún; Bros Peter Gresner, Robert Mrázik and Dominik Svitek as other teachers; Bros Vavrinec Jurák and Kristof Kácer doing household and garden works.

3. Ten scholastics, with Bro. Jaroslav Rybánsky as Director.

4. Bro. Arnost, Visitor, hiding from the police, and some refugees from suppressed communities: Bros Etienne Oravec, Bela Singer, Tichomír Miko, Joachim Pasko, Marián Temes.

To these we must add some five young Brothers who had just finished their novitiate. There was room for all and more, with hopeful prospects for the future but for the fact that the Communists had seized all power and began to use it – an uncivilised, brutal lot.

Some time in April 1950, Bro. Visitor called an emergency council to decide on weighty matters. In case of an imminent danger of the Brothers being arrested, novices, scholastics and young Brothers with only annual vows were to be sent to their families. The time and mode of doing so was left to the discretion of the respective Directors. Then came 3 May, the Patronal Feast of Močenok, and with it a strange episode.

There was much talk about arrests during the evening recreation, but 'no danger for the Brothers for the time being' was the general opinion. Then, like lightning, an absolute certainty struck a responsible Brother: 'They will come tonight.' After night prayers he hurried to Brother Visitor. Result: novices, scholastics, and Brothers with annual vows were told to pack and be off by 10.00 pm at the latest. In the dead of night, secret police, militiamen, protected by police and the military, broke into the Brothers' rooms, roused the quietly sleeping Brothers, gathered them against a wall in absolute silence while they ransacked the house. They were furious to find that the young were gone and wanted them back, but no addresses were given them. The young Brothers were spared the brutal arrest of the professed Brothers, and later, the seductions organised for seminarians and young religious through pretty but shameless girls. Communists always begin with attacks on common decency, and aim at utter lawlessness in morals. They seem to know St Augustine's *Nemo incredulus, nisi impurus.* [There are no unbelievers except the impure. Ed.]

For some time the Brothers in Močenok were given working clothes and worked in the gardens. Later they were mixed with other religious in concentration monasteries, and dispersed throughout the whole country as workmen in dams, factories, woods and the like.

Another episode: At Klicava dam, Bro. Oldrich Elías became a foreman, but refused to do the taskmaster or political whip. He was warned, threatened, and finally sent to Zeliva monastery, a real concentration camp for religious superiors. It took him three days to find out where he was – no communication with others possible. He wrote a note to his parents: He was well, at Zeliva. He handed the note through the fence to the first passer-by, but was seen by the guard and punished. Two weeks on bread and water in a dark, wet cellar without bed. Double pneumonia after a week. The camp doctor declared: 'The man will not hold out; you must shift him to a room.' And the commander retorted: 'No, he must serve his sentence.' And he did, and later gave me an account of it. For his sake I could not speak of it then, but now that he sleeps the sleep of the just in the Klastor-pod-Znievom cemetery, I can.

A word more about the 'Klicava Dam'. It was known as 'The Dam of the Religious', and Zápotocky, then President, came solemnly to open it. 'We thought of teaching you how to work', he said, 'and you have taught us.' The dam was declared 'Model Dam.' A whole group of our Brothers had worked on it.

4. Normal School at Spisská Kapitula

The school was founded as a church institution in 1919. Early after World War I, the Bishop of Spisská Kapitula, Dr Ján Vojtassák, who too got acquainted with the FSC Brothers in his travels abroad, invited the Brothers in Slovakia to teach at his normal school and have their young Brothers trained there. The Brothers gladly accepted this generous offer and sent there Bro. Dezider Oravec to teach Mathematics, Physics and Chemistry, and Bro. Etienne Orfavec to teach German and Handicraft. At the same time Brother scholastics were given a chance to study at the normal school and to live in community in the seminary. Gradually more Brothers gave lectures at the normal school along with priests. In 1946 the whole school was given to the Brothers and Bro. Marián Temes was appointed Director, helped by Brothers Pankrác Dobrovodsky, Alojz Vrone, Andrej Pitoniak, Zdenko Halcín, Joachym Pasko and Apolinár Danis. Some lecturers were priests, and the seminarists continued to attend the lectures as did our scholastics. Their director was Bro. Pankrác Dobrovodsky.

The school did very well and pleased his Excellency, the Bishop, who often visited both the school and the Brothers' community. The Brothers, on their part, and, for that matter, the whole of East Slovakia loved their great Bishop. Of course, they reaped the hatred of the enemy of all good. By the end of 1949, the oldest normal school of the former Austrian-Hungarian empire had to be handed over to Communist school management, to the immense loss and grief of Slovakia. The Brothers found refuge in other communities, Močenok in particular.

The Bishop himself was guarded day and night by hundreds of brave men, and the 'authorities' dared not to touch him. Then he said to his faithful defenders: 'My good people, you have much to do; go to your work.' Hardly were they away than a great force came to arrest the Bishop.

At the sad news people wept and the Bishop's voluntary guards lamented, 'Why did we yield to our good Bishop and leave him alone?'

He was judged in the Communist fashion and sentenced to long years of forced labour for having 'exploited the people' and for an interminable array of 'crimes against the people', and when amnestied at the close of his life of suffering, he was secretly transported to a private house in Bohemia, so much did the 'authorities' fear his very appearance in public. His death was not announced, and yet thousands came to pay their last respects to his mortal frame. Bishop Vojtassak's memory is and will be cherished by the Slovak nation, along with Bishops Buzalka and Gojdic, and we hope that the Church will one day place them on her altars.

Brother Marián's father was secretly dragged away into the forest during the 'Slovak rising' in 1944, and there bestially murdered by the partisans, who, soldiers apart, were a set of scoundrels.

5. Reformatory at Slovenská Lunca

Originally, this was a state institution accommodated in an old medieval castle dominating the upper Hron valley. The reformatory was rather a failure, and in 1939 the Brothers were asked to take it in hand.

First they had to select suitable apartments, tidy them up and adapt them to meet the requirements of a well-conducted corrective. The largest and best hall on the first floor was made into a chapel, cleaned, furnished and decorated. Then came the classrooms and other apartments carefully chosen and put in a good state. Surroundings claimed attention too. Extensive waste land was changed into playing fields, gardens and orchards. More than a thousand trees were planted by the boys, who, fond of novelties and tickled by the appearance of their new educators, readily lent a helping hand in making their 'boarding school' as pleasant looking as possible. This was already part of their re-education, and disposed them to respond to the efforts of the Brothers. These insisted on personal cleanliness, good order everywhere and on work well done. The boys were given ample opportunities to choose their work after lessons, to take part in sports and games, to have hobbies and even to continue their studies at secondary and high schools, though the majority learnt some trade of their own choice.

A judicious choice of the Brothers for this institution was imperative:

Director: elderly and experienced Bro. Etienne Oravec, tolerant and fatherly. Teachers: Bros Belo Singer, long-standing teacher, very good pianist; Matej Krupa, trained for the work, a gentleman, clever at puppet work and stage play, loved by all; Benedik Brezan, experienced teacher, disciplinarian, later Director; Viliam Paulis, accountant; Anzelm, an enthusiastic teacher and conductor of brass music; Rufin Lences, all-round tailor – made smart uniforms for the boys, dresses for puppets and actors, liturgical ornaments.

Each Brother excelled in something or other and made himself popular with the boys and very acceptable in the community. The institution earned the reputation of a very good 'boarding school'; nobody spoke of delinquents or of a reformatory. These successes roused the jealousy and ill-will of a certain Rev. Chabada. An investigating commission found his accusation false, but the end of the institution was at hand. In 1948 it was taken over by the state. Great disorders ensued and the institution was suppressed.

The Brothers joined other communities and shared their lot of 1950. Brother Matej Krupa was mobilised for military exercises, after which he was allowed to find employment as best he could. One day in 1958, as he was cycling to the little town of Detva, a lorry knocked him down dead, perhaps on purpose, for

Bro. Matej exercised a good influence on the young. The driver was not prosecuted.

5. Primary School at Zákamenné

In 1938, two Brothers, Tichomír Miko and Ondrej Odrobiniak, took over the management of a mixed primary school at Zákamenné, birth place of the great Bishop Ján Vojtassak, at his request. Board and lodging were offered them by the poor but generous parish priest, Ján Balara. The school consisted of three separate buildings with seven classes taught by three women and four men teachers. The Brothers were welcome and readily merged with the simple folk whose social, cultural and religious activities they shared to raise them to a higher level. But their privileged work was teaching Catechism, leading the children to holy liturgy and preparing them to receive the sacraments, First Communion in particular.

In 1938, an old spacious school, all in wood, now empty, was given to the Brothers. They made it a cosy home. The Bishop had a new school and community buildings erected in the years 1941-1944 and lower secondary classes were added in 1946. But the Communists were impatient to seize power and start inculcating their perverse and perverting ideas. Forcibly they sent to the school their own creatures who spoke and acted as the simple people had never seen or heard before.

In 1950, the Brothers' community of four, with Bro. Jozef Paluch as Director, escaped arrest and the concentration camp because their community had not been registered. They were, however, not allowed to teach.

7. Normal School at Bánovc

This Institution was created at Dr Jozef Tiso's urgent appeal to the 'high school office' in 1933. Lectures started in August 1934 with Dr Tiso as Director. Out of 160 appllcants only 40 could be admitted for the first year's course. Then 40 more students were added every year to make the total number of students 160 in the fourth year and ever after. In 1937 Dr Jozef Tiso asked Bro. Arnost, Provincial of the Brothers, for two Brothers to act as prefects and as 'training teachers' at the annex primary school. At the 'teachers academy' they taught Didactics and Methodology. They used to have their meals with the chaplains; on Sundays with Dr Jozef Tiso, later President. The last couple of Brothers teaching at the Academy were Bro. Ladislav Chrenka and Bro. Karol Suba, who taught there until 1949. Some 400 Catholic teachers came out of the Normal School or Academy.

Approximate statistics for 1950

Brothers in communities: 65

Scholastics: 10

Novices: 6

Junior novices: 25

Statistics for December 1989

12 Brothers

Claiming to be a Brother but without vows: 1

Over 80 years of age: 7

About 75: 3

Under 70: 2

Localities where Brothers' graves are cared for:

Bubenec, Moravec, Sladeckovce, Močenok, Ruban, Bác.

CHAPTER EIGHT

Some Remarkable Brothers

W*e are indebted to Brothers Dominic Bernhard, Tiberiù Ratu and Ján Rybansky for the first-hand informa-tion they have provided for us about the Brothers in Romania and the former Czechoslovakia. There are other Brothers whose names have already appeared in various chapters who deserve at least a slightly longer mention of their lives because of the ways in which they embod-ied in so many ways the Lasallian ideal of 'brotherhood'. Their lives can continue to inspire us.*

Brother Atanasiu Motica[21]

Born in Circilau in Transylvania in 1914, the fu-ture Brother Atanasiu finished his secondary schooling at 18 years of age with the Brothers in Oradea and, sponsored by the Greek-Catho-lic parish priest of Oradea, made his novitiate in Vienna in 1932-1933. For his scholasticate he re-turned to Oradea where he graduated four years later with his Master's degree. In 1937-1938 he taught at St Josef in Bucharest before being required to undergo military service,

---

[21] Material from a note in Spanish by Brother Francisco Martin in the archives of the Brothers' community in Iasi, Moldova.

where his exemption from combat as a religious led him to be given the rank of sergeant as a basic instructor in language and practical matters.

Having taught briefly at Craiova with the Brothers, he was twice again called to the army, in 1939 as Sub-Lieutenant and in 1942 as Captain. It was while serving at Odessa as liaison with the German army that he used to walk several kilometres into Odessa each morning to attend Mass at a Latin-rite church. There were usually two or three German officers who came by car to this same Mass.

One morning, when it was raining heavily after Mass, the German officers invited Atanasiu to ride with them. In the back seat, seated between two officers, someone remarked that he must be a fervent Catholic to be walking into Mass each day. When Atanasiu replied simply, *'Ich bin Schülbruder'* [I'm a Christian Brother], one of the German officers said, 'So am I. What are you doing here?' Thus, unexpectedly, Atanasiu made the acquaintance of Brother Ansbert Reichert from Illertissen, serving like him as a conscripted non-combatant. Later, the two Brothers were able to meet up with some Romanian Brothers in Bucharest.

Atanasiu, in recounting this incident, remarked that he seemed to have a special 'guardian angel' to get him out of difficult situations. After 1948, when the Brothers had been confined to the major seminary in Bucharest, he was arrested in 1951 when the Italian church in Bucharest where he had worked as sacristan and choir master was closed down by the authorities. Atanasiu found himself confined in a small room with about 30 people to await further examination. It so happened that he needed desperately to go to the toilet, but at first his request was denied. Atanasiu noted however that the guard spoke with the distinctive accent of the Carpathians near Brazov where he himself had been born. He therefore remarked to the guard,

'You come from Brazov, don't you?'

'Yes', said the guard.

'So do I', said Atanasiu.

'What are you doing here?' asked the guard.

'I don't know', said Atanasiu. 'I've got nothing to do with these other people here.'

'Go', said the guard, so Atanasiu did!

It was this quickness of spirit, of adapting to whatever situation in which he found himself, that led Atanasiu in 1953 to follow a course and become qualified as a repairer of radios. He continued his work as catechist and choir organiser in the Saint Josef cathedral until 1959 when he was arrested with the remaining nine Brothers still at liberty and exiled to Olariu with two younger Brothers. These two eventually left the community but the resourceful Atanasiu began working in the market gardens and organising the export of produce to markets. He had to report to the local *Securitate* every Saturday ('I realised they were more frightened of me than I was of them', he would comment, laughing), but used the money he gained to buy a typewriter and began to translate books and articles from French and German into Romanian.

In 1962, obliged to be confined within a three kilometre radius of his residence, he became interested in the levelling and balancing of farm lands, lived with three local farming families and in 1969 qualified in front of a jury of five agricultural experts as a Topographical Engineer. This gave him a steady income and he became a lecturer in the Agricultural School of Calarasi (1970-1971).

After 1972 he was allowed to become the administrator of a rest home owned by the Catholic bishop of Bucharest at Sinaia, not far from his birthplace. It was here that he ran youth clubs for young people, taught religion in many families, formed and directed a parish choir, and, with his carefully hidden second typewriter in the cellar, increased his translation and diffusion of books and articles to sustain the faith of the various groups with whom he worked. The District *Rundbrief,* 1994, No. 1 has a photo on page 7 showing all these books as they are now gathered in the community archives at Iasi.

In 1990, he was at last free to form community at Oradea with Brothers Marcellin and Damian in an apartment provided by the Greek-Catholic bishop. In 1992 he came with other Brothers to form the community at Iasi as is described in the final chapter of this Memorandum.

Brother Justin Nohai (1920-1976)[22]

As is described in the overall chronicle about Romania, Brother Justin at just 30 years of age was arrested after the Communist invasion of the Nunciature on 19 July 1950, cruelly tortured over a period of 20 months in prison and eventually condemned to 25 years forced labour on the Danube-Canal. During his time in prison in Bucharest, he was closely associated with a number of the Greek-Catholic (Uniate) bishops imprisoned there, and indeed had one of these bishops die in his arms.

Released as part of the Amnesty of 1964, he was, as remarked elsewhere, severely weakened by his 15 years of torture and forced labour, and never again regained full health. When he was finally treated in a hospital in Vienna after 1990, the doctors could still find marks of the electrodes with which he had been tortured. He lived his final years in communities in Vienna, sometimes a little unstable in his mind, but faithful and prayerful to the last

[22] From the memorial card in the Strebersdorf archives.

Brother Augustin Iosif Cicu [23]

As described in the chronicle of chapter 2, Brother Augustine was arrested in August 1958, imprisoned and interrogated, and condemned to 15 years forced labour in the show trial of 17 December 1958. He survived the Danube Delta, was able to return to Bucharest where he had relatives, and after 1967, as responsible for the finances of the Catholic archdiocese in Bucharest, was able to live in the Chancellery up to and after his compulsory retirement in 1977.

After having had a number of requests to be treated in a clinic in Vienna denied, he was eventually granted a visa during the winter months. To receive the visa, however, he was told to attend a certain office and to make sure that he brought his overcoat. After some time, his overcoat was returned to him with the visa and he was told that on his arrival in Vienna he was first to go to a certain address. Here the overcoat had to be handed over to someone and later returned to him. He became aware, of course, without being told, that he was smuggling something, but he was to say nothing. He received his medical treatment, but when he applied some years later for a return visa to Vienna, it was somewhat cynically pointed out to him that this was impossible because, on a previous trip, he had been a smuggler!

Brother Augustine's position at the Chancellery in Bucharest was eventually the safest and most secure link between the Austrian Brothers and the Romanian Brothers, as he was able to look after foreign currency brought by visitors and distribute it as needed. He acquired his aunt's house after her death, although he did not live there, and it was there in 1988 that I was able for the first time to meet all the Romanian Brothers who

---

[23] I was privileged to meet Brother Augustin on a number of occasions and to listen to his story.

came together one evening for about two hours when I brought them copies of the 1987 Rule in French and German.

A charming man, Brother Augustine was loved by all who came to know him. He died in the Chancellery in 1994.

Brother Bonifazius Sattmann

Brother Bonifazius Klemens Sattmann, born in 1891, joined his older brother Jakob in the formation program in Strebersdorf from 1905-1911 and for 50 of his life as a Brother taught in Romania. As Romania entered the war on the Allied side during the first World War, he was interned for 18 months and suffered a similar fate in the second World War, being interned under the Russians after 1944. Brothers Dominic and Tiberiù vie with one another in appreciating the importance of his leadership after the closure of the schools in 1948. Here comments from their separate accounts in chapters 5 and 6 are put together:

> Brother Boniface (Bonifazius) was bursar and superior at a difficult time. His trust in Providence impressed us all and gave us courage. None of us was either faint-hearted or cowed, even if this was not always easy. He was the father, the leader and everybody's friend despite his deafness. He prayed a lot precisely because he was deaf. After the grace of God, it was to him that we owed our community life. He was the superior that Providence had prepared for us and given us for those troubled times. The number of Brothers who were free diminished. Calm Brother Bonifazius, however, exercised a strong influence on his Brothers. Each of us had to indicate his agreement [i.e., about staying or leaving. Ed] or disagreement in writing. The Brothers, and especially Brother Bonifazius, directed these activities. The Brothers languishing in prison were not forgotten. When there was a renewal of vows, each

Brother had a candle with his own name and Brother Bonifazius said the formula for those who were absent. At table, on solemn occasions, a place was set with the name of the absent person. Everyone present had to say: 'You too may find yourself one day among the absent.

It is clear from Brother Dominic's account of his interrogation in August 1958 [see chapter 5] that the Communist authorities also had come to realise the important leadership role played by 'the old fox' Brother Bonifazius.

On 24 April 1959, the Communist authorities banished Brothers Bonifazius, Silvester and Julius to enforced obligatory residence in the Franciscan monastery of Estelnic near Brazov. It was from here after the amnesty of 1964 that Brother Bonifazius was allowed to return to Austria. As is suggested elsewhere, however, it was this first-hand contact and the information brought by the repatriated Brothers that built on this initial visit. The success of this visit prompted successive visits from Brother Liebhard, Provincial, and the provincials that followed him.

Brother Bonifazius died at 84 and was buried in the Brothers' cemetery in Strebersdorf. Brother Klemens Ladner, a compatriot from the same village, gave a warm and thoroughly deserved tribute to this old deaf man, this quiet leader, who had undoubtedly inspired and encouraged his Brothers in their time of greatest need by the quality of his own dedicated life, truly a Brother to his Brothers.

Brother Tarcisiu Rata

If 'the blood of martyrs is the seed of the Church', the life and suffering of Brother Tarcisiu Rata, seems to have been a particularly inspiring example for all the Romanian Brothers. Brother Tarcisiu came from the Siebenburgen part of Transylvania where the Greek Catholic church was uncompromising in its attachment to Rome. The unsigned account of Brother Tarcisiu's life and death in *Rundbrief* (1978, No. 1, pp. 6-7) emphasises that it is not accidental that just as the martyrdom [sic] of four Greek Catholic bishops who died in prison after their various arrests after 1948 was aimed at destroying any connection to Rome, so too was the arrest and torture of Brother Tarcisiu in 1950 for having communicated this news to Rome from the Nunciature in Bucharest.

Brother Tarcisiu was born in 1917 in Satu Mare, entered the juniorate of the Brothers at Oradea in Romania, made his novitiate in Maria Laubegg (Austria) in 1934, and received his teacher's diploma in 1938 after studies in Oradea. He began teaching in Bucharest but in 1942 had to join the army where he served with distinction as an officer on the Eastern Front against the Russians, credited with saving the life of a Hungarian general. From 1945 to 1950 he served as the executive head of the Nunciature. As already indicated in the various chronicles, he was arrested along with a Sister and two other Brothers, tortured and condemned to 25 years imprisonment. Even in prison, his instinctive leadership qualities came to the fore. He was greatly respected because he refused to allow fellow prisoners to be ill treated.

He was reprieved under the 1964 amnesty and allowed to return to enforced residence near Bucharest. During his 14 years imprisonment, Brother Tarcisiu renewed his annual vows each year, so that it was only in 1967 that he was able to make his final profession. His death on 27 November 1977 at only 60 years of age not only brought most of the surviving Brothers in Romania together, but provided the occasion for many people whose lives he had touched to come together for a most impressive funeral. Brother Bruno Schmid, the newly named Provincial of Austria, visiting Romania for the first time, was deeply impressed by this funeral and it became the launching pad for his own extraordinary personal mission on behalf of all the Brothers in Eastern Europe.

Brother Liebhard Maria

Brother Liebhard, who appears at various times in the chronicles on Romania, was born in the Austrian Burgenland in 1915. He entered the Brothers in 1932, completed his professional training in the summer of 1936 and began teaching in the St Andreas school in Bucharest in the same year. He was recognised officially for his mastery of the Romanian language.

In 1943 he was conscripted into the German army, and became a prisoner of the Russians for some time, before managing to get himself returned to Austria. He served as teacher, and then Director of the school in Bad Goisern, where he made a significant contribution to the updating of the geological history of Upper Austria by his discovery of significant fossils in the nearby mountains. Provincial from 1958 to 1967, he was a delegate in Rome at the important General Chapter of 1966-1967, following the Second Vatican Council.

Meanwhile, because of his personal knowledge of Romania and his deep interest in what had happened to the Brothers, he began early in 1964 a series of journeys behind the Iron Curtain, usually accompanied by a young Brother skilled in car maintenance because of the precarious state of the roads, especially in Romania. These journeys were risky and he had several experiences of being closely followed and interrogated by the *Securitate* in Romania and of prolonged hold-ups and searches at border crossings between Romania and Hungary and Hungary and Austria.

It is undoubtedly to Brother Liebhard that the credit must go not only for his personal engagement in helping the Brothers of his own District in Hungary and Romania, but also for his ensuring that the General Council of the Institute became better informed and ready to help as required. The subsequent prolonged commitment of the Austrian District was sparked by Brother Liebhard.

I was privileged on three occasions in the summers of 1988-1989 to accompany Brother Liebhard in his retirement years on mountain walks around Bad Goisern and to hear his personal stories of his visits behind the Iron Curtain. For parts of the overall chronicle, and for some particular stories not previously written, I am indebted to these conversations with Brother Liebhard. He remained an indefatigable walker to the end when, suffering from Alzeimher's disease, he lost his life trying to cross a flooded river not far from the Brothers' retirement home *Maria Laubegg* in Southern Austria.

Brother Bertrand Fetter

Brother Bertrand Fetter, who succeeded Brother Liebhard as Provincial in 1967, continued the support to the Brothers in Hungary and Romania. As he did not have his predecessor's advantage of speaking Romanian, he made use of the experience gained by the twin brothers Walter and Heribert Pingizter as chauffeurs and guides during the visits he made. He was generous in supporting Brother Augustin Cicu's medical visit to Vienna and in obtaining money and medicine for the Brothers forced to live alone.

Brother Severin Hegedüs [24]

Born in what was then northern Hungary (today, Slovakia), the young Ernst Hegedüs, fluent in Hungarian and German, entered the Brothers in Austria in 1925. After serving in various schools in Vienna as a teacher of German, Mathematics, History and Shorthand, he returned to Hungary in 1938. He was in the community of St Josef in Budapest XII throughout the Second World War, including the siege by the Russians.

The general chronicle in chapter 4 leaves no doubt that he was the enterprising leader responsible for the saving of the Jewish families and for helping the German Brothers to escape from the siege. As already indicated in chapter 4, Brother Severin was deported from Szeged before eventually being able to find his way back to Budapest. After negotiating his return to Austria in 1959, he held different leadership positions in two of the schools within Vienna. During his retirement in *Maria Laubegg*, 1994-1998, he wrote a very carefully researched series of articles, published in the District *Rundbrief*, which is the definitive history of the Brothers in Hungary.

Brother Bruno Schmid

Born in Austria in 1933, the young Bruno Schmid as a boy of 12 following the Anchluß was asked to sit an exam to qualify to receive special training for Hitler Youth. He recalls his father taking him to one side to tell him that if he passed the exam he would never be welcome to the family again. He failed, and continued to fail

[24] Material taken from his memorial card.

each further attempt to enrol him. Having entered the Brothers after completing the *Gymnasium* in Strebersdorf, Brother Bruno made his novitiate in the international novitiate in Bordighera in northern Italy.

Following a highly successful period as a student at the Vienna university, Brother Bruno became a distinguished educator honoured as such by the Austrian Government for his outstanding work as Principal of the high school and *Gymnasium* at Strebersdorf. In his role as Provincial of the Austrian, Hungarian and Romanian province (1977-1986), as Brother Tiberiù's chronicle in *Rundbrief* (1998, No. 1, page 7) notes, 'Brother Bruno came to Bucharest for the funeral of Brother Tarcisiu. By this opportunity, Brother Bruno and the Romanian Brothers came to know one another. In the summer of 1978, Brother Bruno brought the Vicar-General Brother John Johnston to Bucharest … and for the next 18 years, Brother Bruno paid a visit at least once each year, and after 1990 made many more visits.'

My work of liaison as a member of the General Council between 1986 and 1993 enabled me to make about 12 visits by car with Brother Bruno, especially to old Brothers living with their families or in aged-care institutions in Moravia and Slovakia, as well as to Brother Demeter in the Osek monastery in Bohemia. I came to admire his gentle courtesy, especially the way in which even without being able to address people in their own language, he communicated his love for them and his interest in them. Often, one aspect of these visits was to bring medicines requested by Brothers or families during a previous visit, and he never failed to find out in his own discreet way how they were placed with regard to money. He was always unfailingly courteous to the officials who were in charge of the centres where some Brothers were still confined .

Another aspect of these visits for me was to see quite a

number of Brothers in care centres or in families who often had their original *Manual of Piety*, the Brother's prayer book prior to the 1950s, on their bedside table. I especially recall one Slovak Brother who never failed, as we went to leave, to take the prayer book in his hands and to show it to us as though to remind us that he was united with us in his daily prayer.

As Provincial of the newly-created District of Central Europe in 1994, Brother Bruno was the moving and guiding spirit in the re-establishment of Lasallian works in Romania, Hungary and Slovakia. In his *Essai Historique: Suppression et Reconstruction du District de Tchécoslovaquie*, Brother Vincent Gottwald mentions Brother Bruno's presence and active support sometimes seven or eight times on a single page, and certainly with reference to practically every important decision.

Brother Bruno's untimely death and burial at only 63 years of age brought tributes from a wide range of people representing important positions in Church and State in Austria, as well as Archbishop Joan Robu of Bucharest, as reported in *Rundbrief*, 1986, No. 1, pp. 1-7. The tributes paid to him crown the efforts of all those Brothers and friends of the Austrian District who reached out to their Brothers in Eastern Europe in so many ways between 1948 and 1989.

Brother Vincent Gottwald

It would be difficult to exaggerate the importance of Brother Vincent Gottwald in the restoration of a Lasallian school and community in Slovakia. Born in 1916 in Moravia, he joined the Brothers to become a missionary. He made his novitiate in French in 1933-1934 at Lembecq-les-Halles in Belgium, at that time the centre of the

Institute, and followed this with a scholasticate in Dover, England. With other Brothers from Central Europe, he went to Sri Lanka where he taught in the capital, Colombo, and eventually became Director of a school with over 3000 pupils. After the Second World War, he followed the second novitiate in Rome in 1947, did further studies in England and Ireland, and became Visitor of the District of Colombo in 1956. As such he was a delegate to the 1966-1967 General Chapter.

Following the Chapter, he was asked to found the Institute's Central Secretariate to support missionary activity (SECOLI), and linked the Institute with the United Nations groups of FAO and UNESCO. He was involved in 1979 in the setting up and financing of Bethlehem University of which he eventually became the archivist. It was from here in 1990, at 74 years of age, that he accepted the call to help re-found his original District after 43 years of Communist rule.

His account of what was achieved in the next three to six years is astonishing. Even in his summary account (pp. 4-20) in his *Essai Historique: Suppression et Reconstruction du District en Tchécoslovaquie*, it is difficult to find a week where he was not on the road somewhere, or in England or in Rome or in Vienna, meeting civil or church authorities, finding a solution to a nonfunctioning heating system, drawing up plans, meeting with architects and builders and education authorities.

Brother Vincent died in Vienna at 80 years of age. It was my privilege to represent the world-wide Institute at his burial in the Brothers' cemetery at Maria Laubegg on 24 February 1996. I say 'represent' because former students, parents, Brothers from Sri Lanka, India and Pakistan would like to have been there; so too would so many thousands of young people who had benefitted from the schools founded through his foundation and direction of the Institute's missionary fund he had organised; so too the Brothers of the community of Bethlehem university who remembered his presence among them; teachers and students from the recently opened school in Raca were a reminder of the future which Brother Vincent had helped create. He had lived and shared his 'brotherhood' with all these people to the end of his life as he lived out the vows he had professed – 'to go wherever I may be sent, to do whatever I may be asked to do'.

Brother Klemens Ladner

Brother Klemens Ladner, Visitor of the Austrian District 1986-1995, continued to support the Brothers in Eastern Europe throughout his period in office. He lived the joy of being able to invite Brothers to Vienna after the collapse of Communism. He was responsible for the negotiations with the Spanish Region that brought Spanish Brothers to Romania to learn the language, re-found communities and finally open the school at Pildesti. Following the death of Brother Bruno in 1996, Brother Klemens succeeded him as Visitor of the enlarged District of Central Europe.

CHAPTER NINE

'Being Brothers to One Another'

T he text which follows is the foundation text, the anthropological cornerstone on which John Baptist de La Salle's institute was constructed. It is worth reflecting on what the author, De La Salle's biographer, Jean-Baptiste Blain has written, because it is a statement of *identity*, the distinguishing mark of the Brother's vocation, just as *Ora et Labora* (Pray and work) is for Benedictines or *Ad majoram Dei gloriam* (For God's greater glory) is for Jesuits.

Reading and pondering this text is, I suggest, the key to understanding why the Communist suppression of the Brothers' works in Eastern Europe generated an almost instinctive reaction among the Brothers, not only in the countries where their works were suppressed, but also in nearby counties that remained free. This can be best understood in terms of their unique understanding of brotherhood as being 'brothers to one another' as members of a community, but also 'brothers to the young' who, as De La Salle wrote so often to his followers, are 'confided to our care'. The importance of this concept was perceived by De La Salle's first biographer, Jean-Baptiste Blain in the following text.

Brothers of the Christian Schools

Blain describes how the first teachers chose a new name: Brothers of the Christian Schools

The adoption of the new garb brought about a modification in the name of the Community. The name 'Brothers' was the one that fitted them best, so they chose it, leaving the name schoolmasters to those who perform this function for pay. Humility and charity suggested giving up that name; it had not even been fitting for men who professed to run schools only so that Jesus Christ might reign in them and so that they might teach Christian doctrine gratuitously. If the name schoolmasters had been acceptable up to this time in a house where uniformity of lifestyle and equality in all things had not yet bound the subjects together and where some of them were still vacillating in their vocation, it was no longer proper now that they had joined together to form a single body. Consequently, the name Brothers truly belonged to them, a name which nature gives to children who share the same blood and the same father on earth and which in religion describes those who have the same Spirit and the same Father in heaven.

In this way, the name Brothers of the Christian and Gratuitous Schools became thenceforth the official name of the children of De La Salle. From now on, we shall call them by no other. This appellation is the correct one because it includes the definition of their state and indicates the mission proper to their vocation. This name reminds them that the charity which gave birth to their Institute must be its soul and life, that it should govern all their deliberations and animate all their projects, that it should inspire all their decisions, rule all their undertakings, govern all their words and deeds. This name teaches them the excellence of the duty they have assumed, the dignity of their state, and the holiness proper to their profession.

It tells them that as Brothers they owe each other mutual

proofs of tender but spiritual friendship and that considering themselves as the elder brothers of the children who come to be taught by them, they should exercise this ministry of charity with truly loving hearts.

[Blain, *The Life of John Baptist de La Salle*, translation by Brother Richard Arnandez, Vol. 2, p. 186]

As already noted in the Preface to this work. this Memorandum brings together important documentation about what was lived in the Districts of Eastern Europe (except Poland) between 1948 and 1990. It sets out to show in some detail 'the brotherly concern shown in so many practical ways by the Brothers themselves amid their own sufferings and the extraordinarily generous and sustained efforts made by successive Brothers Visitors of the Austrian District during all these years.'

Why This Memorandum?

As already noted in the Preface, with the exception of the article of Brother Tiberiù in chapter 6, which was published in French, Spanish and English in the Institute *Bulletin*, No. 235 in 1991, the important story of the way in which a practical brotherhood was lived in Eastern Europe is not sufficiently known to the rest of the Institute, as the principal articles, written in German and Romanian, are not well known outside of the countries where these languages are used. The story of the fate of the Brothers in Czech and Slovakia after 1948 was not documented at all before 1988, and the longer account written in French by Brother Vincent Gottwald in 1993 deals mainly with the period after 1990. As regards Hungary, the savage suppressions that followed 1948 and the aftermath to the premature revolution of 1956 have left only a few traces of what was once a flourishing section of the Institute. Brother Severin's articles in German constitute a complete history, and are an important resource but restricted to those who read the language.

The Gospel image used by Jesus reminds us that the seed has to die before it can produce fruit. The story of the Brothers in Eastern Europe is just such a story because it is essentially a story of brotherhood. It is the story of the way in which so many of the Brothers from the Austrian District, from Spain and from the central government of the Institute, have ensured that in Romania, in Slovakia and in Hungary, there are Lasallian works once again.

The Strength of the Community

In the foregoing narratives of what happened in the various countries under Communist oppression after 1948, the chronicle from Romania is different. The closing of the schools in Bucharest in 1948 that put the Brothers onto the street, ironically gave them the advantage of being confined initially in the former major seminary as their common living area within which they formed a community. The strength of a community of like-minded persons is always stronger than the individuals in it. There was, moreover, a leader. The accounts of Brothers Dominic (chapter 5) and Tiberiù (chapter 6) both emphasise the importance of the leadership of Brother Bonifazius:

> Soon the Brothers were looking for work; individual or
> group lessons in family homes. This state of affairs faced the
> Brothers with very complicated problems, but as mature and
> experienced men they found solutions. From morning until
> night without any respite, by tram, bus or on foot, in rain and
> snow, they went about Bucharest. After their travels, seated
> around tables, their conversations sounded like academic ar-
> guments because they brought ideas, impressions and news
> from every corner of the capital. In spite of it all, the Brothers
> continued to meet in the Major Seminary where Brother Bon-

ifazius, their Director and Auxiliary-Visitor, welcomed them
with open arms. The two Brothers' communities merged into
one under the leadership of the Director and Auxiliary-Visitor, Brother Bonifazius Sattmann. There were about 20 of us.
Each of us had to indicate his agreement or disagreement in
writing.

Brother Bonifazius was bursar and superior at a difficult
time. His trust in Providence impressed us all and gave us
courage. None of us was either faint-hearted or cowed, even
if this was not always easy. He was the father, the leader and
everybody's friend despite his deafness. He prayed a lot precisely because he was deaf. After the grace of God, it was to
him that we owed our community life. He was the superior
that Providence had prepared for us and given us for those
troubled times.

Some friends advised the Brothers to be more careful
because of spies, but dear Brother Bonifazius feared nothing
and gave the Brothers courage.

It is not surprising, therefore, that the *Securitate* themselves
eventually saw, as in the document on Brother Dominic's interrogation (chapter 5), that the leadership of Brother Bonifazius
and the access to a common meeting place strengthened the
Brothers in spite of their dispersal. After the arrest of Brothers
Dominic, Tiberiù, Augustin and Florentin in 1958, the *Securitate*
effectively banished the remaining nine Brothers from Bucharest into three separate groups of three.

By comparison, the Brothers in Czechoslovakia and Hungary
found themselves very quickly dispersed, even to some Czech
Brothers being sent many kilometres away into Slovakia, and
Slovakian Brothers being sent away into Moravia or Bohemia.
It is interesting that Brothers Ceslav Dlouiy and Frantisek Demeter were the only two relatively young Brothers who ended up
together in Bohemia in the Cistercian monastery in Osek and so
offered one another mutual support until Ceslav's death in 1976.

In Hungary, the way in which the authorities gradually got rid of anyone who had held an important post while the Brothers were still in charge, ensured that very little of the preceding Lasallian spirit was preserved. As the reference to the original idea of separating the Brothers' community from the school by a wall in Budapest XII shows, the aim was to break all links to the past.

After 1964

The amnesty in Romania that eventually repatriated Brothers Bonifazius and Sylvester to Austria and eventually led to the liberation of Brother Dominic, was the starting point for the enormous involvement of the Austrian Brothers, through successive provincials to the present day. There is little doubt that the 'debriefing' of Brothers Bonifazius and Sylvester after their return to Vienna gave the first full account of what had happened, and what was still happening in Romania. The Provincial, however, Brother Liebhard, a fluent Romanian speaker, with his own experience of living in Romania from 1938 through to his liberation from the Russians in 1946, had already visited Romania early in 1964 with Brother Walter Pitzinger, an expert car mechanic, ostensibly to effect a 'cure' in the Carpathien mountains, not far from where Brothers Bonifazius, Silvester and Julius had been confined in the Franciscan cloister at Estelnic.

Brother Liebhard seems to have been able to move as he wished, because he had supplied some money to the local police chief. On arriving at the Franciscan cloister late at night, however, the gatekeeper either did not hear the bell or decided to ignore it, so the young Brother Walter eventually climbed over the wall and opened the gate so that the Austrian car would not be visible from outside.

It is difficult to discover just how many journeys Brother

Liebhard made, but his fluency and his detailed knowledge of the country certainly helped him to move freely at a time when the Communist policy everywhere demanded that local people report any contact with foreigners An overview of what this brotherly support from a succession of Austrian Provincials eventually became can only be hinted at in the following summary account taken from Brother Tiberiù's account in *Rundbrief*, 1998, No. 1, pages 8-9 and from some District Council minutes. The information is not always complete, however, as it needs to be remembered that at this time Brother Tiberiù was still under close personal surveillance and usually unaware of what was happening elsewhere.

> Shortly after the amnesty early in 1964, Brother Provincial Liebhard came from Vienna to visit Brothers Justin and Tarcisiu. The following year he came once again at Easter and in August he came once again to meet with the relieved Brothers. And he did not come empty-handed … Aware of the very difficult circumstances in which the Romanian Brothers were, the Provincial attempted to have the Austrian government interested in offering help.[25] The Romanian government, however, categorically refused this suggestion.

> The minutes of the Austrian District Council meeting for Saturday 23 November 1968 record that

> *Brother Provincial Bertrand Schönberger and Brother Walter Pingitzer flew to Bucharest to bring our Brothers the new Rule, Mass books, three metres of cloth, shaving gear and medicines. Brother Provincial was able to speak to the Brothers briefly about the District and the Institute. On 26 November they returned to Vienna. On 27 November, Brother Provincial Bertrand and Brother Walter drove to Budapest to bring gifts to the Brothers. This visit was greatly appreciated.*

---

[25] Possibly by having the Romanian Brothers admitted into Austria?

Once it was known in what difficult circumstances the Brothers were, Brother Provincial used his authority to make sure that the Austrian Brothers felt it an honour to do whatever they could to help. The Romanian Brothers came under this category. As time went on, the Brothers began to follow a more settled way of life. The Securitate, however, from time to time felt they should inquire about the 'health' of the Brothers when so many Brothers were making these visits behind the 'Iron Curtain' concerned about visiting their friends. They therefore[26] applied some pressure: 'Are you hoping to organise something new? Do you still hope to resume the kind of life you lived before 1948? Don't rely on false hopes that will come to nothing. Get married and forget the past. Believe us in making you aware of this less stressful way of living.'

To make things easier, the *Securitate* posed no problems to the Brothers finding positions. Almost all the Brothers found work, except Brother Justin whose health was ruined because of the treatment he received during his 15 years of imprisonment.

In his role as Provincial of the Austrian, Hungarian and Romanian province, Brother Bruno came to Bucharest for the funeral of Brother Tarcisiu. By this opportunity, Brother Bruno and the Romanian Brothers came to know one another. In the summer of 1978, Brother Bruno brought the Vicar-General Brother John Johnston to Bucharest and then in 1986, 1992 and 1996 Brother John visited as Superior General. For the next 18 years, Brother Bruno paid a visit at least once each year, and after 1990 made many more visits.

In the 1980s the surveillance was slightly less rigid. In 1983, Brothers Atanasiù and Tiberiù were able to spend a month in Vienna. In 1984 and in 1989, Brothers Marcellin and Atanasiù visited Vienna and Rome. In 1989 Brother Tiberiù spent two months at CIL in Rome. Brother Damian made his first visit to Vienna in 1990.

---

[26] After the visitors had left.

After 1991, the next Brother Provincial Klemens Ladner and [the German] Brother Engelbert Dunkel maintained this link with the Romanian Brothers to keep up the contact. On the occasion of a feast or thanksgiving day, the visits of these higher Superiors brought some Brothers together and provided the opportunity for prayer and discussion to their mutual benefit. Even the elderly Brothers from Satu Mare were not disappointed.

In his account of the symbolic importance of the opening of the community in Rusovce, Brother Vincent Gottwald details the different sources of finance, furniture, chapel ornamentation, garden tools and writing material for the school offered by the various Districts of the Central Europe Region and comments that 'it was a touching gesture, in a fraternal spirit of encouragement to us for the reconstruction of the District ... the Delegation as well as the school at Raca owe a permanent debt of gratitude to these different benefactors.'

As is mentioned elsewhere, Brother Bruno Schmid for almost 20 years was ready to help in any way he could. This was especially so in his work with Brother Vincent Gottwald in his attempts to re-launch the Brothers' community in Slovakia. For example, on page 5 of his Essai, Brother Vincent notes that 'on 25 April [he] was able to organise himself materially with regard to having a car available, a typewriter, a photocopier, etc. This necessary equipment had been obtained in Vienna, thanks to the help of our Brothers in Strebersdorf.'

It is worth noting that although the Austrian District was responsible for Romania and Hungary, the former Czechoslovakian District was a separate foundation not only in a political sense but also in terms of language. But these differences vanished overnight: they were Brothers, and the Austrian District showed to a remarkable degree just how important was their common brotherhood by their generosity in supporting the reconstruction of communities in Slovakia after 1990.

Finally, there would be no school in Raca today nor three communities of Brothers if it had not been for the generosity of the Polish Brothers in sending three young men to learn the language and to dedicate themselves to a new beginning.

Being Older Brothers to the Young

The second half of Blain's explanation as to why the first teachers chose to call themselves 'Brothers' is expressed by him thus:

> that considering themselves as the elder brothers of the children who come to be taught by them, they should exercise this ministry of charity with truly loving hearts.

This sense of 'relationship as 'older brother' is complementary to but inseparable from the sense of 'being brothers to one another'. It is not surprising, therefore, that, in spite of the difficult circumstances in which individual Brothers found themselves, they instinctively sought to express their identity as Brothers in sharing faith with others.

The general chronicles given in previous chapters and the personal narratives of Brothers Dominic Bernhard, Tiberiù Ratu, Jan Rybansky and Severin Hegedüs all reflect a deep sense of their *identity* as Brothers. This is shown by the way in which, after the closure of their schools and institutions, finding themselves unable to continue their former role as teachers and catechists, they instinctively sought other ways of continuing to be 'brothers' to young people and to adults. It is sufficient to recall how the Romanian Brothers in Bucharest, shut out of their schools in Bucharest and forbidden to wear their religious habits, gradually developed an extensive catechetical work in parishes and in the formation of some of their former pupils as youth leaders (see chapter 2). Key to this was undoubtedly the calm leadership of Brother Bonifazius, recognised in the personal narratives of Brothers Bernard and Tiberiù.

The same concern is shown in the way in which Brother Marcellin, having survived the work on the Danube Canal, lived after 1964 in a hut in the garden of the English Sisters outside Bucharest and found a way of teaching music to the 'unofficial' novices in their vacation house where the Sisters had been moved after they had to vacate their convent. Later, after resuming his work as organist at the Saint Teresa church, he acceded to the requests of families to teach religion to their children, only to be betrayed and returned to prison. As I have noted in my first meeting with him in 1969 (see chapter 1), he was already calculating how to resume the work as soon as possible by buying a bicycle.

Brother Atanasiu's personal contribution to sustaining Christian faith can be found today in the community archives at Iasi where there are over 100 books and carbon-copies of articles which he translated into the Romanian language from French or German and circulated in his own clandestine apostolate. It was with great glee that he spoke about visits he had received from the *Securitate* to compare the impression of his typewriter with copies of religious articles that had been discovered without the police ever discovering the carefully hidden second typewriter in the cellar on which he did his carbon copies. He mentioned that he was even plagiarised when he later found one of his books published under someone else's name! I recall that when I asked him in 1990 in Vienna why he took such a risk, he answered with great simplicity that it was at least something he could do to sustain the faith of people suffering persecution.

Brother Severin's narrative of the siege of Budapest and of

the role of the community in finding food and shelter for Jewish families is so matter-of-fact that it is easy to forget that he and the other Brothers were risking their personal safety and indeed their own lives in what they were doing. Notice too that, after being allowed to return to Budapest after his confinement in Debrezin, he speaks quite naturally of making acquaintance with some of the Catholic families in the area and gradually taking 'the evening meal with various families who wished him to instruct their children in religion' (see chapter 4).

After I had renewed acquaintance with Brother Ján Rybansky in Bratislava after 1986 where he taught English to small groups of students, I discovered that his English teaching was always 'mixed' with discreet teaching of the Catholic faith to his students. When I met two of his former students in 1990, they both acknowledged the debt they owed to their teacher for the careful instruction in faith which he had shared with them and eventually with their families.

Two Examples of Brothers Preserving Their Identity

As already indicated, the dispersal of the Brothers in Czech and Slovakia was total. Following the period of forced labour, there was no possibility to come together so that for Brothers in temporary profession, their vows lapsed. Some finally professed Brothers eventually consulted priests about their status and received advice that allowed them to be released from their vows. But there were other Brothers who always felt that they were Brothers and wished to remain so.

I was able on two occasions to visit the famous Osek Cistercian monastery in Bohemia where initially two Brothers, Ceslav Dlouhy (see chapter 3) and Frantisek Demeter, were confined and required to work the farm and produce the food necessary to feed the Sisters of 51 different congregations who were confined there. I remember that on my first visit in 1987 with Brother Bruno Schmid, the woman who was in charge was quite formal with us and left no doubt that she knew that we were 'Brothers' and we could meet Demeter for a short time, but he had work to do and our visit should not be long. On the second occasion, however, in May 1989, she apologised that Demeter was needed to drive her to a doctor's appointment, but we could have access to the library – a world-famous library – where Czech university students were making an inventory of the books. As an aside, I can mention that my presence was useful because a number of students brought books to me for me to identify them as Latin or Greek!

When Demeter returned, Bruno took the opportunity to speak with the woman because he had discovered that she had just been diagnosed with cancer, so Demeter and I were left alone. As he spoke only Slovak, we asked one of the Sisters who spoke German to be our translator. What Demeter said to me was translated, but at first I could not understand what he meant. He said that he was grateful that we had come to see him and brought him money, but he did not know whether or not he was really a Brother. What he was saying, I realised, was that as he had never had the opportunity to make his final profession and as his temporary vows had lapsed long ago he was not really a Brother!

When I realised what he was asking, I asked him why he had spent 42 years here in the monastery when he was really free to go if he did not want to be considered a Brother. I embraced him and assured him that he was indeed a Brother. With the collapse of Communism some months later, arrangements for Demeter's final profession were made in the following year. On 12 November 1990, a large number of Brothers from Czech and

Slovakia, from Austria, Holland and Belgium made the journey to Osek for a celebratory Mass in the splendid Baroque chapel where the Sisters used all their musical skills in honouring this man who had been faithful all these years in serving others, and who had already lived what he now professed.

Earlier, on 28 July 1990, there was another example of a former novice who had remained faithful since 1948 and lived out his brotherhood alone. Brother (Dr) Severin Pitoniak had continued to study and had gained advanced degrees while still cherishing the desire one day to rejoin the Institute. It was decided that he should first pass some three months in the novitiate in Poland as a renewal program, but he was allowed to make annual vows in the presence of all the Brothers now forming the new Delegation.

A further example of what the Brothers had contributed both as a community and as individuals was the celebration held in July 1992 by men who had been trained as teachers at the *St Ján pod Skalou* normal school in Prague. Nearly one hundred former students, many of them long retired, came together to honour the memory of the men who had trained them and to express their hope that the Brothers would one day be able to re-launch this work in their country.

CHAPTER 10

After 1990

The Challenges in Czech and Slovakia

The story of the Brothers in Hungary, Romania, Czech and Slovakia following the collapse of the Communist governments
is the story of attempts at restoration of Lasallian 'human and
Christian education' as the Brothers' Rule of 1987 defines itself,
against the background of the impact of some 42-43 years of
Communism. History has shown again and again that what is
often called the 'emigré' mentality of those who knew a pre-
Communist state and survived the collapse of Communism,
tends to seek and try to restore exactly what was lost. But this
is to forget that the generations of these 42-43 years had never
known the society in which their parents, or, more usually, their
grandparents lived.

A practical example of this in 1991 was the attempt of a religious congregation of women to take over their convent again
and administer a school which was handed back to them in Bratislava. The young Sisters of some 40 years ago were in their
early 20s when they were confined in concentration convents
and monasteries, so it was perfectly natural for them to wish

to restore the kind of girls' school they had known. Their well-meant attempt, however, to impose the traditional hats, gloves and uniforms of convent schools from another era was met with downright refusal not only by the girls themselves but also by their parents, before a compromise was reached and a lay woman installed as the principal.

In the case of the Brothers, there were some Slovak missionary Brothers, trained in French in Belgium before the Second World War, who had spent their lives teaching in French in Lebanon. They were contacted by Brother Vincent Gottwald, and indicated that they were keen to return to help when the Brothers were offered a school at Raca near Bratislava. But the Slovakia to which they returned – and in which they had never taught in their own language – was so different from what they done so skilfully in other lands that they quickly realised that their contribution would have to be much more through their presence and example rather than through the overall administration of a secondary school. There was another very important and subtle difference: the Slovak language which these dedicated men from the countryside had spoken in their young teens sounded almost archaic to secondary school pupils used to contemporary speech and usage as heard through television and radio.

The Return of Properties

It was perfectly natural for the Brothers to wish to have returned to them the various properties to which they had the title deeds. Among the reasons for wishing to do this was the fact that there were elderly Brothers without any income or with only a small pension which was barely adequate for them to exist, and the ownership of these properties could provide the financial basis for the work of what was now known in the Institute as a Delegation.

This presented Brother Vincent Gottwald with a series of very delicate problems. In Prague, for example, the former teachers' college, *St Jan pod Skalou*, with its extensive grounds, lake and park, had become a recreational area for the citizens of Prague. There were only a few elderly Czech Brothers still alive and the attempt to restore this property to private hands would be difficult to justify on many levels. It was decided, therefore, to hand over the original documents of entitlement to the city of Prague. The Brothers did, however, regain ownership of the Joanneum in the centre of Prague, kept an apartment for the use of the Visitor of what is now the District of Central Europe when he has occasion to visit Prague, and arranged for the Salesians to administer the home as a hostel for young men.

In Slovakia, the Bojná property presented an equally delicate problem. The Brothers had the original title deeds, but a local Communist official had illegally constructed a small factory in the middle of the property which gave steady employment to around 20 people from the local area. While it was agreed that the factory was built without permission, any attempt to have the factory closed and removed would not make the Brothers welcome in an area where people were struggling to make a living. Lawyers eventually negotiated a compromise solution which restored the *legal person* of the Brothers, recognised the ownership of the property and established an annual payment for the use of the property.

Re-opening of Communities

Brother Vincent Gottwald's first concern after his appointment in 1990 to lead the Delegation of Czech and Slovakia was the opening of a community. As is indicated elsewhere in this Memorandum, it was the utter destruction of the communities that left the Czech and Slovak Brothers isolated from one another and from all that the community could offer in terms of support and direction. The example of Brothers Ceslav Dlouhy and Frantisek Demeter working together in Osek for so many years is a story of what might have been elsewhere.

The opening of the community was achieved when the District of Poland offered three young Brothers to learn Slovak so as eventually to help establish a Lasallian school in Bratislava. A property for the community was found at Rusovce, some 16 km south of Bratislava, and eventually purchased with money supplied by the General Council in Rome, Brother Bruno on behalf of the Austrian District, the District of North Belgium, and the Visitors of Europe after Brother Vincent had met with the General Council in Rome to establish a program of foundation. As Brother Vincent acknowledges, 'it was a very moving gesture, offered in a fraternal spirit of encouragement for the reconstruction of the District' (page 11). From particular communities and schools in Europe, there came as well furniture and equipment for the community and for the school.

The community at Rusovce was formally established with four Brothers on 9 February 1991 in a liturgical ceremony presided at by the Archbishop of Traava, in the presence of the Brother Superior General, John Johnston, Councillor Gerard Rummery and Brothers from Poland, Austria and Belgium. Presentations prepared in English and other languages had already been translated into Slovak and other languages so the ceremonies could be understood. Some former Brothers whose vows had elapsed because of the impossibility of meeting to renew them, were also present at the ceremony.

Towards the end of 1990, Brother Jan Rybansky had suffered the amputation of a leg but the prosthesis he was offered was unsatisfactory. He had originally wished to stay in the apartment he had occupied in Bratislava where he had friends and former students to support him, but it was eventually thought better for him to go to Vienna where a much more satisfactory prosthesis was made for him. He returned to Rusovce as a member of the community until his death in August 1993. Three more elderly Brothers died before the end of the year.

De La Salle School, Raca

The school at Raca was blessed and opened with a lay director and administrator on 2 September 1991. The official name of the school is *Zakladna Skola Jana de La Salle* (Elementary School John de La Salle): it is recognised as a school of the De La Salle Brothers, administered by them, and with all salaries and administration costs paid by the Slovak Republic. The Ministry of Culture and the Ministry of Education sent representatives to the opening and praised the Brothers for their rapid response to the new order. Before the school year began, the staff had gone through workshops that gave a rapid exposure to recent documentation on the Catholic school and the particular emphases of a Lasallian school.

But, as the Brothers had to travel some 25 km from Rusovce by public transport, it was obvious that a second community was needed closer to the school. This was eventually opened on 15 May 1991, with five Brothers, including the three from Poland, because the government, through the Ministry of Cultural Affairs, was allocating money to religious communities that had not been compensated for lost properties. In the meantime, Brother Vincent had been able to arrange for extensive publicity about the Brothers and their historical contribution to their country to be arranged and broadcast, both through radio and television. A short life of Saint John Baptist de La Salle in German had been translated into Slovak by Brother Severin and a thousand copies printed. Brother Paul Grieger, based in Rome for many decades, had translated a number of his many writings into Slovak, but a major effort at translation was needed to bring more contemporary documents into the Slovak language.

In November 1993, a third community was opened at Presov. Some interest had been shown in the Brother's life after the radio and television broadcasts. There had been two young men who initially underwent some formation as Brothers but who did not stay. The Brothers were no longer well-known as before, so it was decided that two Brothers would work as a pastoral team, speak in many parishes and youth groups, work with young people and explain priestly and religious vocations as a means of attracting young people to something they had not previously known or experienced.

In all this activity, Brother Vincent's account contains references to the support of Brother Bruno and that of Brother Klemens Ladner, the Austrian Provincial 1986-1995, as well as to the continuing financial and pastoral support from the General Council in Rome. By July 1992, Brother Vincent was exhausted and was replaced as Delegate by Brother Etienne Lenicky returning home from Lebanon. Brother Vincent, at the invitation of Brother Bruno, retired to Vienna where he prepared his *Essai historique*. Following his death on 19 February, 1996, he was buried in the Brothers' cemetery in *Maria Laubegg*.

The Skola Jana de La Salle at Raca today includes a full primary school and a full secondary school or *Gymnasium*.

Re-opening in Budapest XII

Two former students of the Brothers took the initiative in order to return the Brothers' school at Budapest to their care. Both had not only studied at the original school in Budapest but had also completed matriculation through the Brothers' school in Strebersdorf in Vienna. Peter Hertelendi and Imre Vörös, both with distinguished careers in law, worked with the Hungarian government so that the Brothers could again take charge of their property which was being used as a school for training young people in national dance.

The standing of Brother Bruno with the Austrian government authorities and the steps taken, especially by Professor Vörös, resulted in an agreement between the Austrian and Hungarian governments whereby the school would, as previously, from kindergarten to matriculation, be taught in both Hungarian and German, and would be funded by both governments. It was on these conditions that the school was formally returned to Brother Gerard Rummery, representing the Institute, and, as was emphasised, *not* to the Catholic Church, which was in prolonged negotiations over the return of sequestrated property.

The school opened in September 1995 under the guidance of Alfred Bryctha, formerly Director of the Lasallian school in Schopenhauerstrasse in Vienna, and Gabriele Hampel, and is known as the *Österreichisch-Ungarische Europa-Schule* (Austrian-Hungarian European School). From kindergarten to matriculation, classes are taught in Hungarian and German with English also forming part of the basic curriculum. Teachers from Austria receive their salaries from the Austrian government, teachers from Hungary from the Hungarian government. At the time of writing, the school has proven itself and is well established with 500 students.

Romania after 1990

It was in Holy Week of 1990 that all the Brothers from Eastern

Europe were invited to a three day conference at which the Brother Superior General John Johnston and Brother Council- lor Gerard Rummery would discuss with them some possible paths to the future. There was no question of the return of prop- erties as the Brothers had never owned their schools in Romania but had worked for their local Church. From Romania, Brothers Atanasiu, Damian, Marcellin and Tiberiù were in attendance. The group of Spanish Districts that made up the ARLEP Region had already been in dialogue with the General Council and had agreed to invite Brothers to volunteer to come to Romania to learn the language and to help re-launch the Lasallian mission there. Earlier discussions between Church authorities and the Romanian Brothers had suggested that the three Catholic vil- lages of Pildesti, Gheraesti and Tamaseni in the diocese of Iasi were the most likely sites where vocations to the Brothers' life might be found, and it had been suggested that s school in Pild- esti would be the most suitable site.

By September 1991, the first three Brothers arrived in Iasi where Brother Francisco Martín took on the post of Reader in Spanish at the University Joan Cuza while the others began to study the Romanian language in a language school. Two more Brothers arrived in the following year and on 31 July 1993, the first robe-taking ceremony in 51 years took place at Mass in Tamaseni in the presence of Bishop Petru Gherghel of Iasi, when Daniel Ciobanu and Iosif Beda were received as novices in the presence of about 4000 people.

Meanwhile in Oradea, the Greek-Catholic Bishop Hossu pro- vided a residence for a new community where Brothers Damian, Atanasiu and Marcellin eventually came together by September 1992 to teach in the pedagogical seminary of the Greek-Catholic diocese. Brother Tiberiù came in 1995 to the Iasi community as a teacher of German and of Religion and History.

All of these activities were sponsored by the General Council of the Institute in Rome, the Spanish Region and the Austrian District through the support of Brother Klemens Ladner as Provincial, and by the continuing work of Brother Bruno Schmid through his personal contact over many years with Archbishop Robu of Bucharest and Bishop Gherghel of Iasi. With the creation of a new District of Central Europe in 1995, comprising the former sectors Austria, Germany, Hungary, Romania, Czech and Slovakia, Brother Bruno was again named Provincial.

It was on 25 October 1998 that the newly-constructed school, *La Salle,* was opened in Pildesti by Bishop Petru Gherghel of Iasi, in the presence of government representatives and Brothers from Romania, Austria, Spain and Rome. Following the advice of local people and give the particular needs of rural communities, the co-educational school offered the core educational subjects plus a wide range of practical subjects for boys and girls, including woodwork and metalwork for boys, sewing and dressmaking for girls, and computer studies and secretarial skills.

Once again, it was a practical demonstration of international 'brotherhood', something that could be achieved because of the generosity of the Spanish Region in appealing for volunteers and for its financial support, from the continuing financial support offered by the Austrian Brothers and from the guarantee provided by the central government of the Institute. It was, symbolically, the recognition by the Institute that the sufferings and sacrifices of generations of Romanian Brothers were not in vain. It was a new beginning.

Sources

Sources consulted have been provided from the De La Salle Archives of 476 Via Aurelia, Rome, through the resident archivist, Frère Francis Ricousse. Through the courtesy and professional cooperation of SR Karl Gerzabek at the De La Salle Provinzialat Archives in Strebersdorf, Vienna, I have been given access to all original documents and manuscripts concerning the former Districts and Sub-Districts of Czechoslovakia, Hungary and Romania. References to these and other sources are acknowledged throughout the text. Brother Johann Gassner, Provincial, has been most helpful through his personal assistance and through the expertise provided by his secretary, Gabrielle Mannersdorf, in preparing the photos used in this document. Translations, unless otherwise acknowledged, are by Brother Gerard Rummery.

Krähen und Pelikane [Crows and Pelicans]. Written in German in Vienna at Christmas 1965 by Brother Dominic Bernhard only a short time after his release and arrival in Vienna. The text, over 7000 words in length, reads like a prolonged meditation as the author, some months after being freed, begins for the first time to reflect on the six years of forced labour in the Danube Delta and all kinds of memories appear. Four different sections have been translated and incorporated into the general chronicle (chapter 2) and the third section of chapter 5.

Der Heroisch Kampf des Schulbrüder in Rumänien [The heroic struggle of the Brothers in Romania]. Typewritten copy written in Vienna in German in February 1966 by Brother Dominic Bernhard, published in *Rundbrief an die Lasallianische Famile der Schulbrüder*, 1990, No. 1. This complete text has been translated as the basic chronicle for chapter 5.

Eine Fährt ins Blaue [A Journey into the Blue]. Written in German in Vienna in February 1966 by Brother Dominic Bernhard. Sections describing his arrest, his interrogation and his condemnation have been translated and incorporated into the general chronicle and into chapter 5.

Rumänien 1948: Beginn der Langen Nacht von 42 Jahren [In Romania: The long night that lasted 42 years]. Written in Iasi, Romania, by Bruder Tiberiù Ratu in August 1991. Published in French, English and Spanish in the *Bulletin of The Institute of the Brothers of the Christian Schools*, September 1991, No. 235. English translation by Brother Allen Geppert.

100 Jahre Schulbrüder in Rumänien: Eine Kurze Geschichtliche Darstellung der Aktivitäten der Schulbrüder [100 years of the Brothers in Romania: A short history of the activities of the Brothers. Written by Brüder Tiberiù Ratu. Published in the Austrian District's *Rundbrief*, 1998, No. 1. Translated into German by Brother Matthäus Plattensteiner. Certain sections have been translated into English especially in chapter 9.

FSC District of Czechoslovakia. Brother Jan Rybansky's simple account in English begun in 1988 at my request and eventually sent from Vienna by Brother Bruno Schmid after the document had been given to him in Bratislava.

Essai Historique : Suppression et Reconstruction du District de Tchécoslovaquie. Wien, Institution de La Salle, 1993. A 20 page booklet written in French by Frère Vincent Gottwald.

Die Schulbrüder in Ungarn. A complete history of the Brothers in Hungary from its origins written by Brother Severinus Hegedüs has appeared in German in successive *Rundbriefen* of the Austrian District: 1990 -1, pp. 11-6 & 17-21; 1990-2, pp. 7-9; 1991-1, pp. 17-21; 1991-2, pp. 18-21; 1992-1, pp. 22-25; 1993-1, pp. 12-18; 1993-2, pp. 18-21.

The *Rundbrief* has been the official Bulletin published by the Brothers in Austria two or three times each year for over the past 50 years.

Interrupted Lives: Catholic Sisters under European Communism. A DVD presentation made in USA which explores the experiences of Sisters in Ukraine, Lithuania, Slovakia and Hungary between

1948 –1989 through interviews with survivors. Three historians offer comments on important details.

The Calvary of Romania, Robert Royal, Catholic World Report, March 2000.

In the Archives of the Brothers' community at Iasi in Romania, I was able to consult documents and see photographs referring to the history of the Brothers in Romania. There are collections of recent photographs taken since 1990.

Personal Interviews

On Saturday 28 and Sunday 29 August 2010, in Pildesti, Romania, I was able to converse once again with **Brother Marcellin Joan Magui**, 89 years of age, whom I had first met in 1969 (see chapter 1). Still very lucid in recalling details of his own life, Brother Marcellin was particularly helpful in describing some of the different pastoral activities of the Romanian Brothers around Bucharest between 1948 and 1959.

On two occasions, in September 2010, I was able to converse with **Herr Walter Pingizter**, who as a young Brother with skills in servicing and maintaining cars (a necessary skill, given the state of the roads in Romania), accompanied successive Provincials, Brothers Liebhard and Bertrand, and other Brothers, in more than 15 visits behind the Iron Curtain. He also presented me with some personal documentation of these visits.

On two occasions in September 2010, at Strebersdorf, I was able to discuss the renewal of works in Slovakia, Hungary and Romania after 1990 with **Brother Klemens Ladner**, who, as Visitor, was responsible for the formal arrangements entered into with civil, religious and Institute authorities.

Some of the Brothers in the present **Strebersdorf community** at one time or another accompanied one of the Austrian District Provincials in visits to Romania or Hungary or Czechoslovakia. I had the opportunity to converse with them informally about these visits.

www.ingramcontent.com/pod-product-compliance
Lightning Source LLC
Chambersburg PA
CBHW021128020426
42331CB00005B/670